Dorothy S. Becvar, MSW, PhD
Editor

The Family, Spirituality and Social Work

The Family, Spirituality and Social Work has been co-published simultaneously as *Journal of Family Social Work,* Volume 2, Number 4 1997.

Pre-publication REVIEWS, COMMENTARIES, EVALUATIONS . . .

"**T**he *Family, Spirituality and Social Work* boldly and in-structively invites us into the world of a social worker's efforts to engage with spirituality in therapy in its many forms from constructivist to Christian to women's spirituality and more."

Harry J. Aponte, MSW
Associate Clinical Professor
Allegheny University
of Health Sciences

Director
Family Therapy Training Program
of Philadelphia
Philadelphia, PA

More pre-publication
REVIEWS, COMMENTARIES, EVALUATIONS . . .

"This thoughtful and thought provoking volume covers a variety of issues and perspectives related to spirituality in family life and family therapy . . . Provides stimulating reading and practical suggestions for practitioners who want to be sensitive to spiritual issues."

Ingeborg E. Haug
Clinical Director
and Assistant Professor
of Marriage and Family
Therapy Education
Fairfield University
Fairfield, CT

"Educators, clinicians and students will appreciate this scholarly, comprehensive and inspiring overview on the integration of spirituality into holistic clinical practice. It provides a theoretical, empirical and practical overview of important issues, ranging from the ramifications of spirituality on family well-being to potential problems that clinicians may encounter when addressing spirituality in practice. Only through the integration of spirituality and counseling can we hope to succeed in our pursuit of excellence in clinical practice.

This work represents a major contribution to our understanding of spirituality and religion within a holistic framework of social work practice. It provides the diverse, yet unified, perspective of authors who have impressive expertise in clinical practice, theory development and research. I applaud their well-written, thoughtful reminder on how we need to honor the spiritual values and experiences of our clients."

Cynthia A. Loveland Cook, PhD, RN, ACSW
Associate Professor
School of Social Service
St. Louis University

"**T**his edited volume by Dorothy S. Becvar focuses on spirituality in social work practice. Most of the eleven contributors, including Becvar, note that spirituality and religious issues have been at the margins of social work practice. Therefore, this edited volume aims to center spirituality and religious issues in therapeutic social work practice. This volume's chapters are diverse in content, with some chapters outlining a framework for incorporating spiritual and religious content and others conceptualizing practice models. Attempts are made to address the meaning of spirituality to Christians . . . this edited volume is a breath of fresh air for social workers that have long felt the need to incorporate spiritual and religious issues into social work practice. This edited volume is timely for the field of social work. Although there are several popular works that emphasize the role of spirituality and religion as meaningful aspects of people's lives, this book is one of the few that speaks directly to social workers about these issues. The book is essential reading for professionals and students who are truly interested in including spirituality and religious issues in practice. It will be a useful supplementary text for teaching about spirituality and religion in courses on family therapy and cultural diversity."

Letha A. Chadiha, MSW, PhD
Associate Professor of Social Work
George Warren Brown School
of Social Work
Washington University
St. Louis, MO

The Family, Spirituality and Social Work

The Family, Spirituality and Social Work has been co-published simultaneously as *Journal of Family Social Work,* Volume 2, Number 4 1997.

The *Journal of Family Social Work* Monographs/"Separates"
(formerly the *Journal of Social Work & Human Sexuality* series)*

Social Work and Child Sexual Abuse, edited by Jon R. Conte
and David A. Shore*

Human Sexuality in Medical Social Work, edited by Larry Lister
and David A. Shore*

Homosexuality and Social Work (available in softcover
from The Harrington Park Press as *With Compassion Toward
Some: Homosexuality and Social Work in America*),
edited by Robert Schoenberg and Richard S. Goldberg*

Feminist Perspectives on Social Work and Human Sexuality,
edited by Mary Valentich and James Gripton*

Social Work Practice in Sexual Problems, edited by James Gripton
and Mary Valentich*

Human Sexuality, Ethnoculture, and Social Work, edited by Larry Lister*

Adolescent Sexualities: Overviews and Principles of Intervention,
edited by Paula Allen-Meares and David A. Shore*

Intimate Relationships: Some Social Work Perspectives on Love,
edited by Wendell Ricketts and Harvey Gochros*

Infertility and Adoption: A Guide for Social Work Practice,
edited by Deborah Valentine*

Sociological Aspects of Sexually Transmitted Diseases
(available in softcover from The Harrington Park Press
as *Decade of the Plague: The Sociopsychological
Ramifications of Sexually Transmitted Diseases*),
edited by Margaret Rodway and Marianne Wright*

The Sexually Unusual: Guide to Understanding and Helping,
edited by Dennis M. Dailey*

Treatment of Sex Offenders in Social Work and Mental Health Settings,
edited by John S. Wodarski and Daniel Whitaker*

Adolescent Sexuality: New Challenges for Social Work,
edited by Paula Allen-Meares and Constance Hoenk Shapiro*

Sexuality and Disabilities: A Guide for Human Service Practitioners,
edited by Romel W. Mackelprang and Deborah Valentine*

Cross-Cultural Practice with Couples and Families,
edited by Philip M. Brown and John S. Shallett

The Family, Spirituality and Social Work, edited by Dorothy S. Becvar

These books were published simultaneously as special thematic issues of the
Journal of Family Social Work and are available bound separately. Visit Haworth's website at http://www.haworth.com to search our online catalog for complete tables of contents and ordering information for these and other publications.
Or call 1-800-HAWORTH (outside US/Canada: 607-722-5857), Fax: 1-800-895-
0582 (outside US/Canada: 607-771-0012), or e-mail getinfo@haworth.com

The Family, Spirituality and Social Work

Dorothy S. Becvar, MSW, PhD
Editor

The Family, Spirituality and Social Work has been co-published simultaneously as *Journal of Family Social Work,* Volume 2, Number 4 1997.

The Haworth Press, Inc.
New York • London

The Family, Spirituality and Social Work has been co-published simultaneously as *Journal of Family Social Work,* Volume 2, Number 4 1997.

The Haworth Press, Inc., 10 Alice Street, Binghamton, NY 13904-1580 USA

Cover design by Thomas J. Mayshock Jr.

Library of Congress Cataloging-in-Publication Data

The family, spirituality and social work / Dorothy S. Becvar, editor.
    p. cm.
    "Co-published simultaneously as Journal of family social work, volume 2, number 4 1997."
    Includes bibliographical references and index.
    ISBN 0-7890-0503-4 (alk. paper)
    1. Family social work. 2. Social service–Religious aspects. 3. Family psychotherapy. 4. Psychotherapy–Religious aspects. 5. Family–Religious life. I. Becvar, Dorothy Stroh.
HV697.F349 1998
362.82'8–dc21   97-47663
                                                                                     CIP

INDEXING & ABSTRACTING

Contributions to this publication are selectively indexed or abstracted in print, electronic, online, or CD-ROM version(s) of the reference tools and information services listed below. This list is current as of the copyright date of this publication. See the end of this section for additional notes.

- ***Abstracts in Anthropology,*** Baywood Publishing Company, 26 Austin Avenue, P.O. Box 337, Amityville, NY 11701

- ***Abstracts in Social Gerontology: Current Literature on Aging,*** National Council on the Aging, Library, 409 Third Street SW, 2nd Floor, Washington, DC 20024

- ***Abstracts of Research in Pastoral Care & Counseling,*** Loyola College, 7135 Minstrel Way, Suite 101, Columbia, MD 21045

- ***Applied Social Sciences Index & Abstracts (ASSIA) (Online: ASSI via Data-Star) (CDRom: ASSIA Plus),*** Bowker-Saur Limited, Maypole House, Maypole Road, East Grinstead, West Sussex RH19 1HH, England

- ***Cambridge Scientific Abstracts,*** *Risk Abstracts,* 7200 Wisconsin Avenue #601, Bethesda, MD 20814

- ***caredata CD: the social & community care database,*** National Institute for Social Work, 5 Tavistock Place, London WC1H 9SS, England

- ***Child Development Abstracts & Bibliography,*** University of Kansas, 213 Bailey Hall, Lawrence, KS 66045

- ***CINAHL (Cumulative Index to Nursing & Allied Health Literature), in print, also on CD-ROM from CD PLUS, EBSCO, and SilverPlatter, and online from CDP Online (formerly BRS), Data-Star, and PaperChase. (Support materials include Subject Heading List, Database Search Guide, and instructional video),*** CINAHL Information Systems, P.O. Box 871/1509 Wilson Terrace, Glendale, CA 91209-0871

- ***CNPIEC Reference Guide: Chinese National Directory of Foreign Periodicals,*** P.O. Box 88, Beijing, People's Republic of China

- ***Criminal Justice Abstracts,*** Willow Tree Press, 15 Washington Street, 4th Floor, Newark, NJ 07102

(continued)

- *Criminology, Penology and Police Science Abstracts,* Kugler Publications, P.O. Box 11188, 1001 GD Amsterdam, The Netherlands

- *Digest of Neurology and Psychiatry,* The Institute of Living, 400 Washington Street, Hartford, CT 06106

- *Educational Administration Abstracts (EAA),* Sage Publications, Inc., 2455 Teller Road, Newbury Park, CA 91320

- *ERIC Clearinghouse on Counseling and Student Services (ERIC/CASS),* University of North Carolina-Greensboro, 101 Park Building, Greensboro, NC 27412-5001

- *Family Studies Database (online and CD/ROM),* National Information Services Corporation, 306 East Baltimore Pike, 2nd Floor, Media, PA 19063

- *Family Violence & Sexual Assault Bulletin,* Family Violence & Sexual Assault Institute, 1121 East South East Loop # 323 Suite 130, Tyler, TX 75701

- *Human Resources Abstracts (HRA),* Sage Publications, Inc., 2455 Teller Road, Newbury Park, CA 91320

- *IBZ International Bibliography of Periodical Literature,* Zeller Verlag GmbH & Co., P.O.B. 1949, d-49009 Osnabruck, Germany

- *Index to Periodical Articles Related to Law,* University of Texas, 727 East 26th Street, Austin, TX 78705

- *INTERNET ACCESS (& additional networks) Bulletin Board for Libraries ("BUBL") coverage of information resources on INTERNET, JANET, and other networks.*
  - <URL:http://bubl.ac.uk/>
  - The new locations will be found under <URL:http://bubl.ac.uk/link/>.
  - Any existing BUBL users who have problems finding information on the new service should contact the BUBL help line by sending e-mail to <bubl@bubl.ac.uk>.
  The Andersonian Library, Curran Building, 101 St. James Road, Glasgow G4 0NS, Scotland

- *Linguistics and Language Behavior Abstracts (LLBA),* Sociological Abstracts, Inc., P.O. Box 22206, San Diego, CA 92192-0206

(continued)

- *Mental Health Abstracts (online through DIALOG),* IFI/Plenum Data Company, 3202 Kirkwood Highway, Wilmington, DE 19808

- *PASCAL, %₀ Institute de L'Information Scientifique et Technique. Cross-disciplinary electronic database covering the fields of science, technology & medicine. Also available on CD-ROM, and can generate customized retrospective searches. For more information: INIST, Customer Desk, 2, allee du Parc de Brabois, F-54514 Vandoeuvre Cedex, France (http//www.inist.fr),* INIST/CNRS-Service Gestion des Documents Primaires, 2, allee du Parc de Brabois, F-54514 Vandoeuvre-les-Nancy, Cedex, France

- *Periodica Islamica,* Berita Publishing, 22 Jalan Liku, 59100 Kuala Lumpur, Malaysia

- *Psychological Abstracts (PsycINFO),* American Psychological Association, P.O. Box 91600, Washington, DC 20090-1600

- *Referativnyi Zhurnal (Abstracts Journal of the All-Russian Institute of Scientific and Technical Information),* 20 Usievich Street, Moscow, 125219, Russia

- *Sage Family Studies Abstracts (SFSA),* Sage Publications, Inc., 2455 Teller Road, Newbury Park, CA 91320

- *Social Planning/Policy & Development Abstracts (SOPODA),* Sociological Abstracts, Inc., P.O. Box 22206, San Diego, CA 92192-0206

- *Social Work Abstracts,* National Association of Social Workers, 750 First Street NW, 8th Floor, Washington, DC 20002

- *Sociological Abstracts (SA),* Sociological Abstracts, Inc., P.O. Box 22206, San Diego, CA 92192-0206

- *Studies on Women Abstracts,* Carfax Publishing Company, P.O. Box 25, Abingdon, Oxon, OX14 3UE, United Kingdom

- *Violence and Abuse Abstracts: A Review of Current Literature on Interpersonal Violence (VAA),* Sage Publications, Inc., 2455 Teller Road, Newbury Park, CA 91320

(continued)

SPECIAL BIBLIOGRAPHIC NOTES

related to special journal issues (separates)
and indexing/abstracting

❑ indexing/abstracting services in this list will also cover material in any "separate" that is co-published simultaneously with Haworth's special thematic journal issue or DocuSerial. Indexing/abstracting usually covers material at the article/chapter level.

❑ monographic co-editions are intended for either non-subscribers or libraries which intend to purchase a second copy for their circulating collections.

❑ monographic co-editions are reported to all jobbers/wholesalers/approval plans. The source journal is listed as the "series" to assist the prevention of duplicate purchasing in the same manner utilized for books-in-series.

❑ to facilitate user/access services all indexing/abstracting services are encouraged to utilize the co-indexing entry note indicated at the bottom of the first page of each article/chapter/contribution.

❑ this is intended to assist a library user of any reference tool (whether print, electronic, online, or CD-ROM) to locate the monographic version if the library has purchased this version but not a subscription to the source journal.

❑ individual articles/chapters in any Haworth publication are also available through the Haworth Document Delivery Service (HDDS).

The Family, Spirituality and Social Work

CONTENTS

ABOUT THE EDITOR

Dorothy S. Becvar, MSW, PhD, is a Licensed Clinical Social Worker and a Licensed Marital and Family Therapist with a private practice in St. Louis, Missouri. She was formerly a faculty member of the University of Missouri-St. Louis, St. Louis University, Texas Tech University, Washington University, and Radford University. Dr. Becvar has presented workshops and taught courses on such topics as spirituality and family therapy, death and dying, and chronic illness. She has also taught systems theory and family therapy for the Family Resource and Training Centre in Singapore. She has co-authored three books, written many published articles, and is the author of the book *Soul Healing: A Spiritual Orientation in Counseling and Therapy* (1997). In addition, Dr. Becvar is currently an adjunct instructor at the Barnes-Jewish Hospital College of Nursing in St. Louis.

Preface

Working with families is old news for social workers. However, while we may long have been aware of the role of religion and spirituality in the lives of our clients, it is only recently that professional conversations in this area have been permissible. Now that we have reached the point in the development of the mental health professions when spirituality is considered to be an important aspect of our work, the door has opened to a whole new array of discussions. In this volume we present a small sampling of the myriad issues and perspectives which social workers may face and want to be cognizant of given the current interest in and focus on the spiritual domain. For, as social worker and family therapist Harry Aponte has written in his book, *Bread and Spirit: Therapy with the New Poor* (1994), we need to recognize that "therapy can be an enemy or a friend to spirit" (p. 8).

In our attempt to befriend spirit, we therefore invite you to consider the ramifications for families of a spiritual orientation in our work as described in my opening article, "Soul Healing and the Family." We may also ponder along with Tim Thayne the process of "Opening Space for Clients' Religious and Spiritual Values in Therapy: A Social Constructionist Perspective." Milo Benningfield attempts to raise our awareness of some of the possible hazards in his article, "Addressing Spiritual/ Religious Issues in Therapy: Potential Problems and Complications." Joyce Hickson and Andrea Phelps provide a counterpoint to the traditional emphasis on male spirituality with their discussion of "Women's Spirituality: A Proposed Practice Model." The next two articles are derived from research studies. Charles Joanides describes "A Qualitative Investigation of the Meaning of Religion and Spirituality to a Group of Orthodox Christians: Implications for Marriage and Family Therapy." And in her article, "Spirituality as a Form of Functional Diversity: Activating Unconventional Family Strengths," Karen Westbrooks offers a view on various resources, including spirituality, which have been little recognized in the

[Haworth co-indexing entry note]: "Preface." Becvar, Dorothy S. Co-published simultaneously in *Journal of Family Social Work* (The Haworth Press, Inc.) Vol. 2, No. 4, 1997, pp. xiii-xiv; and: *The Family, Spirituality and Social Work* (ed: Dorothy S. Becvar) The Haworth Press, Inc., 1998, pp. xiii-xiv. Single or multiple copies of this article are available for a fee from The Haworth Document Delivery Service [1-800-342-9678, 9:00 a.m. - 5:00 p.m. (EST). E-mail address: getinfo@haworth.com].

xiii

literature. Ray Bardill then provides a focus on "The Spiritual Reality: A Christian World View." Finally, we are invited to consider our behavior as professionals from the perspective of "Giving Good Sermons in Therapy," as described by Thomas Smith, Pamela Valentine and Rebecca Williams.

As you read these articles, the hope is that you will receive not only new and useful information but that you will become aware of both the enormous scope of spirituality and the degree to which our effectiveness as social workers may be enhanced through its inclusion in our work with individuals and the families in which they live.

Dorothy S. Becvar, MSW, PhD

Soul Healing and the Family

Dorothy S. Becvar, MSW, PhD

SUMMARY. This article focuses on families in general, both those we as social workers and other mental health professionals work with and those within which we live. Specifically, the focus is on ways that growth may be facilitated as family members operate according to the principles of acknowledging connectedness, suspending judgment, trusting the universe, creating realities, and walking the path with heart. The ramifications for individuals, families and society of the choice to pursue soul healing, or to undertake consciously a journey toward wholeness, also is discussed. *[Article copies available for a fee from The Haworth Document Delivery Service: 1-800-342-9678. E-mail address: getinfo@haworth.com]*

INTRODUCTION

According to the sociologist Claude Levi-Strauss (1956, p. 284), "Society belongs to the realm of culture while the family is the emanation on the social level of those natural requirements without which there could be no society, and indeed no mankind." In fact, the family and society are inextricably bound up with one another, each the condition for and the negation of the other. And it is the family to which society entrusts the "complex and delicate task" of socialization (Lasch, 1975, p. 33), the

---

Dorothy S. Becvar is a Licensed Clinical Social Worker and a Licensed Marital and Family Therapist in private practice.

Address correspondence to: Dorothy S. Becvar, MSW, PhD, 7349 Dale Avenue, St. Louis, MO 63117 (E-mail: YTJT36A@Prodigy.COM).

[Haworth co-indexing entry note]: "Soul Healing and the Family." Becvar, Dorothy S. Co-published simultaneously in *Journal of Family Social Work* (The Haworth Press, Inc.) Vol. 2, No. 4, 1997, pp. 1-11; and: *The Family, Spirituality and Social Work* (ed: Dorothy S. Becvar) The Haworth Press, Inc., 1998, pp. 1-11. Single or multiple copies of this article are available for a fee from The Haworth Document Delivery Service [1-800-342-9678, 9:00 a.m. - 5:00 p.m. (EST). E-mail address: getinfo@haworth.com].

1

context in which society's norms and values are learned and transmitted. It is the family which is central to the process of identity formation (Weigert & Hastings, 1977), and which engages in "the creation and preservation of the emotional well-being of its members" (Glasser & Glasser, 1970, p. 291). Further, it is the family which is the "institution–perhaps the last surviving one–that functions as a home" (Abbott, 1981, p. 13), Lasch's (1979b) "haven in a heartless world." Hence the view that the family be regarded as "the primary resource for most individuals and society as well" (Zimmerman, 1978, p. 457).

As "the most cherished institution of our civilization" (Frankel, 1963, p. 3) the family has long been the object of considerable debate and concern, and certainly we in the United States have contributed our share to this conversation. According to Featherstone (1976, p. 10), "our pervasive sense of crisis concerning children and the family is quite traditional, being part of a worried national conversation that began in the 1820's and has continued to the present." During his visit to this country during the 1840s, the Frenchman Alexis de Tocqueville "observed that there seemed to be an American obsession with reevaluating and remodeling the family" (Abbott, 1981, p. x). One of the principally recurring themes of this discourse, which continues today, is a consideration of whether or not the family is in crisis, whether or not it is breaking down (e.g., Bronfenbrenner, 1976, 1977; Hall, 1995) or is merely in transition (e.g., Coontz, 1992, 1996; Levitan & Belous, 1981).

Statistics and trends cited over the years in support of both positions have included the following: a great increase in divorce (Butts, 1982) and the fact that there are more than twelve million children under the age of eighteen whose parents are divorced, while approximately one million children a year experience a divorce in their family (The Children of Divorce, 1980); a decline both in the birthrate (Glick, 1975); an increase in the number of people living in the context of single-parent, step-parent, reconstituted, and other alternative family structures (Masnick & Bane, 1980), including a vast number of unmarried couples living together (St. Louis Post Dispatch, 1991); an increase in the age at which individuals choose to marry and/or have children (Swerdlow, Bridenthal, Kelly, & Vine, 1981) as well as increasing numbers of couples who choose to remain childless (The New Baby Boom, 1982); an increase in the number of women in the workplace (Lazar, 1979), particularly those with young children (54% of Children Under 18, 1981); an increase in marriage and remarriage (Butts, 1982); increases in juvenile crime, the rate of illegitimacy, family abuse and suicide in the young (Norton, 1982); a decline in mortality rates and the potentially longer duration of marriages (Sullivan, 1979); divorce becoming more prevalent among the rich (Lazar, 1979) but increasing at a greater rate among the poor (Grand'Maison, 1979); the ostensibly more private nature of the family (Laslett, 1980) and yet, in fact, the more public family whose many original functions have either been taken over or at least have become subject to public surveillance (Lasch, 1979a); and the fact that most people live in families (Levitan & Belous, 1981). Much of the current conversation and controversy comes under the heading of "family values."

I choose to take the position that the many and continual changes being experienced by families are not symptoms of deterioration, but rather are signs of evolution and growth. While not denying that we, both as parents and as a society, are faced with a myriad of problems and challenges, I see, for example, shifts in family form as logical responses in a wider context of societal change, including great advances in technology and the increased mobility it has participated in generating. And I keep in mind the fact that some things never change. For example, we might note the following statement:

> The young people today love luxury. They have bad manners, they scoff at authority and lack respect for their elders. Children nowadays are real tyrants, they no longer stand up when their elders come into the room where they are sitting, they contradict their parents, chat together in the presence of adults, eat gluttonously and tyrannize their teachers.

It is interesting to note that those words were spoken by Socrates, *ca.* 470-379 b.c.

At the same time, however, I also believe that there is much more that we might do in order to facilitate the development of the kind of human beings we would like our children to become as well as the creation of the kind of society in which we would like them and us to be able to live. What I am recommending is a broadening of our focus. For, to paraphrase medical intuitive Carolyn Myss (1997), it appears that families generally are in the business of teaching survival rather than evolution. While I certainly would not abdicate the former in favor of the latter, I believe that we would do well to include an awareness of and an emphasis on evolution as part of the childrearing/familying process. Evolution is, for me, what soul healing is all about.

SOUL HEALING

Soul healing (Becvar, 1997) is my story about a spiritual orientation in counseling and therapy. It refers to the creation of contexts in which the focus is no longer primarily on problems but rather emphasizes solutions and the facilitation of wellness in a holistic sense. Such a context encompasses approaches that enable the client to feel empowered and includes discussions of that which is experienced as meaningful and beautiful. Further, considerations of the religious and spiritual dimensions of people's lives are invited and/or welcomed.

The basic assumptions of my story, derived from both secular and spiritual perspectives, include the following:

1. We live in a constantly conjoined universe in which separateness is an illusion.
2. Each one of us is an aspect/expression of the divine and each of us has an inherent urge toward growth and wholeness.
3. Consciousness is the ground of all that is and mind/nature form a necessary unity.
4. We create our reality as a function of our beliefs and perceptions.
5. Each of us has a desire for meaning and purpose in our lives.

To explain, given a postmodernist orientation, I assume that reality is inevitably subjective, that human beings dwell in a "multiverse" (Maturana & Varela, 1980) which is constructed through the act of observation. In other words, believing is seeing. The idea of minds and objects as separate is deconstructed for if we can only know reality via our perceptions, then that which we perceive is a function of our mental processes, or mind, and thus the two are inseparable. Mind may therefore be understood as non-local, or universal and empowering of all creatures and things.

From such a perspective, facts are replaced by frameworks and the views of all are understood as equally valid. There is no "transcendent criterion of the correct" (Gergen, 1991, p. 111) and the social worker/therapist/social scientist therefore assumes a not-knowing, non-expert position (Anderson, 1993). There is an emphasis on discourse and the role of language as the means by which individuals come to know their world and in their knowing simultaneously to construct it. Indeed, each of us experiences and expresses our knowing through a system of language which has a separate existence.

That is, each of us is born into and assimilates pre-existing forms of language in a culturally created linguistic system. In the process of socialization we learn to speak in accepted ways and simultaneously to adopt the shared values and ideology of our language system. Our words express the conventions, the symbols, the metaphors of our particular group; we cannot speak in a language separate from that of our community. When operating from such a perspective, the goal becomes one of deconstructing "facts" by delineating the assumptions, values, and ideologies upon which they rest and considering ourselves and our constructions about life and living with skepticism and perhaps humor.

It also is understood that the self is constructed in relationship and that the individual is a participant in multiple relationships. What is more, a problem is only a problem as a function of the way it is constructed in certain relationships. Both the self and problems take shape and have meaning in the context of specific relationships and are expressed through the language of the consensual domain within which these relationships occur. There are no decontextualized individuals or problems.

Beginning with respect for individual differences, great emphasis is given to the role of conversation, with an awareness of the co-construction of both problems and proposed solutions. All behaviors, including those considered problematic, are understood as "making sense" or being logical to context. And if change is to occur, then the focus must be on the creation of new contexts in which new behaviors become logical responses.

Assuming the above philosophical framework and derived as well from my spiritual orientation, I attempt to operate according to five guiding principles. These include acknowledging connectedness, suspending judgment, trusting the universe, creating realities and walking the path with heart. And I would suggest that it might be useful to consider the ways in which some of the ideas described by my story might be incorporated into interactions in families. I also would remind us that they may have relevance regardless of whether or not one espouses a particular religious belief system.

That is, the realm of spirituality, as I am using the term, is that of the soul and its process of growth and development, which may be facilitated both within and without the context of a specific religious perspective. A spiritual orientation involves operating with an awareness of a transcendent dimension which provides the context for all relationships, all interactions, all that is, which is understood as interconnected and interdependent. In addition, each aspect of the universe is considered to be an expression of the divine, to be infused with spirit, and thus to be sacred. Given this awareness, one recognizes that life has a larger meaning and purpose related to the growth and development not only of individual souls but also of the soul of the world.

Further, I believe that at some level we participate in the creation of all of our experiences, including our physical and emotional problems. And all of our experiences provide opportunities for learning lessons essential to our personal growth, or for becoming whole at a soul level. While we generally are not conscious of the extent to which we participate in choosing our experiences, I believe that awareness of this participation may empower us to understand the degree to which we can create the realities we desire.

As part of this process I recognize the importance of respecting and valuing each person as well as each experience. For I believe we all are involved in each other's destiny and each of us is walking a path toward the self-realization both of our individual selves and of all. Along this path we have high ideals and at the same time we recognize the limits of what is possible. And we look for our efforts to make a difference in the world. Our function is to facilitate harmony and balance through support of each individual on his or her journey towards the attainment of the specific goals appropriate for him or her.

The urge toward wholeness inherent in each person involves an alignment of the physical with the spiritual and allows the soul, through the individual personality, to manifest its destiny or purpose. Further, while the physical expression, or body, of the individual ultimately dies, soul is understood to exist both before and after physical death. Thus at the deepest level there is continuity, just as at the physical level there is impermanence. And we become aware that acknowledgment and acceptance of our impermanence, or death, can transform our approach to life.

RAMIFICATIONS

Now, let us consider how the principles of soul healing may have applicability for family members and thus for society. First, it is important to be aware that *acknowledging connectedness* stands in stark contrast to the priority given in this society to individualism, independence and autonomy. Nevertheless, I believe we would do well to recognize the value of facilitating an experience of connectedness, perhaps increasing awareness for everyone involved of the meaning to be derived from a sense of the interdependence of all that is as described both by quantum physicists (Capra, 1996) and by those espousing a postmodern perspective. Indeed, as we participate in the creation of such an experience, including greater awareness of the depth of our connections, I believe that we might facilitate an overall sense of balance and harmony. What is more, the family is perhaps the most appropriate context for expressing this principle, given the fact that it is here that most of us experience our most intense and intimate relationships. It is here that the ability to love unconditionally most frequently is expressed. And I believe the sense of connection we may feel with our children, parents and other family members, and they with us, might become a model for what is possible in all of our relationships.

To participate in *suspending judgment* is to facilitate acceptance in a manner that avoids blaming or finding fault. Such an experience can be extremely affirming and meaningful, providing a context that allows for and encourages the unfolding of our greatest potential. That is, while we may not condone specific behaviors, we may choose to maintain an attitude of respect for the basic integrity of the family member. In addition, we may attempt to understand the logic of a situation, including our own behaviors, and work to bring about a change in context rather than seeing a problem as residing within a particular person. Such an attitude may have far-reaching ramifications. That is, when the individual is able to experience guilt without feeling shamed, she or he is able to maintain his or her dignity and self-esteem. Further, when emulated and perhaps generalized to other relationships, real change might be forthcoming, both in individual lives and in the larger society. Indeed, we may recognize that we cannot do just one thing (Becvar & Becvar, 1996) and that our behaviors, whatever they are, inevitably have an impact on and influence the various other levels of the systems in which we and other family members live and operate.

To learn about *trusting the universe* and to experience the miracle of the reality that is available when perceived and created from such a stance may be to access a life-enhancing sense of mystery and awe. Thus, we may enable ourselves and other family members to become aware that information is available to all of us on many levels and we all may learn to honor the more intuitive ways of knowing. In addition, with a story that life does indeed have meaning and purpose and the awareness that we dwell in a larger universe within which our dreams may be realized, we may find the ability to understand and cope more effectively with life's challenges, regardless of their magnitude. Indeed, we may recognize that we are the co-creators of such challenges.

Creating realities means focusing on the degree to which our perceptions and beliefs shape our experience of the world. Perhaps there is no context more supportive of a person's ability to experience his or her own power than one in which it is recognized that each of us has the potential to influence our lives in far more significant ways than generally is acknowledged or believed. Thus, to have an epistemology that has a conscious awareness of itself (Keeney, 1983), to be aware that it is we who participate in the construction of our realities as a function of our beliefs, allows us not only to influence that reality but also to focus on and participate in the creation of the changes we desire.

Finally, helping ourselves and other family members to see the potential of *walking a path with heart*, one which embodies our dreams and enriches our souls, may enable us to bring about change not only in our individual lives but also in our world. For, to walk a path with heart is to participate in the creation of a context supportive of all the behaviors and benefits just enumerated. It also is to become a role model for others about what is possible relative to our personal visions (Sams, 1993). What is more, as each of us achieves a measure of success in attaining our personal vision and realizing our full potential, we may move closer to the spiritual fulfillment and, perhaps ultimately, to the world peace about which many of us dream. In the meantime, as we work toward the accomplishment of lofty goals such as these we may find that we have equipped ourselves in what are perhaps some of the most meaningful ways possible.

CONCLUSION

By way of conclusion, I would like first to wonder "aloud" about what might happen if we were to operate according to these principles in our families and in our interactions with one another. For example, I wonder what kind of society might be created if all of its members acted as though each was involved in the destiny of all. What if we assumed that ours was a connection that existed at a soul level, one that survived death and that involved the entire family of man/woman?

I wonder what kind of society might be created if all of its members understood every experience as somehow making sense and providing opportunities for growth and learning. What if such events as divorce were seen as having a logic? What if we believed that a problem exists only as we define a particular phenomenon as such? What if we were able to accept the diverse frameworks of all as having validity in their given contexts?

I wonder what kind of society might be created if all of its members assumed a basic stance of faith in our selves, in each other, in the universe. What if when we asked for assistance we were able to trust that we would be given what was most appropriate for our growth and development?

I wonder what kind of society might be created if all of its members assumed that they participate in creating whatever reality they are experiencing, both separately and jointly. What if we recognized the power of perception and thus our ability to create solutions, our capacity for self-healing, the potential involved in rewriting our personal stories?

Finally, I wonder what kind of society might be created if all of its members assumed they were walking a path toward self-realization at the highest levels. What would happen if we became aware of the miracles that constantly are occurring around us? What if we each experienced a sense of excitement as we went about doing that which was meaningful?

In response to my wonderings, my hope is that as we behave with family members and with each other in a manner consistent with the above assumptions and principles, their and our experience would include the following:

- a sense of connectedness and the feeling of being accepted, validated, respected and supported.
- the feeling not only that they are being heard but also that they have their own expertise as well as other resources upon which they may draw.
- a clear idea about what it is they would like as well as a sense of what is possible and a feeling of hopefulness about the attainment of their goals.
- an understanding of the degree to which they may influence the creation of their reality as well as information about or perspectives on how to proceed.
- a feeling that healing at a very deep level is being facilitated and that their growth and development, or the unfolding of their vast potential, are being encouraged.
- an experience of the power of love and the feeling of being energized and renewed.

As we think now about the ongoing debate about the state of the family described in the introduction, let us consider the following:

> We either fear that human culture is falling apart, or we can *hold the Vision* that we are *Awakening*. Either way, our expectation is a prayer that goes out as a force that tends to bring about the end we envision. Each of us must consciously choose between these two futures. (Redfield, 1996)

That is, if we believe that we create our reality as a function of our perceptions, that believing is seeing, we must recognize that this holds true not only for individuals but also for families and the society of which they are all a part. And while the approach described herein may seem idealistic, perhaps unrealistic, we might do well to recognize that we just might create the reality we desire were we to embrace in our families a perspective such as that described by soul healing.

REFERENCES

Abbott, P. (1981). *The family on trial*. University Park, PA: The Pennsylvania State University Press.

Anderson, H. (1993). On a roller coaster: A collaborative language systems approach to therapy. In S. Friedman (Ed.), *The new language of change* (pp. 323-344). New York: Guilford Press.

Becvar, D. (1997) *Soul healing: A spiritual orientation in counseling and therapy*. New York: Basic Books.

Becvar, D., & Becvar, R. (1996). *Family therapy: A systemic integration*. Boston, MA: Allyn & Bacon.

Bronfenbrenner, U. (1976). The family: Who cares? *Human Ecology Forum, IX* (3), 1-5.

Bronfenbrenner, U. (1977). Nobody home: The erosion of the American family. *Psychology Today*, May, pp. 41-47.

Butts, S. L. (1982). Marriage and divorce totals. *Family Therapy News, 13* 5, 6.

Capra, F. (1996). *The web of life*. New York: Anchor Books.

The Children of Divorce, (1980). *Newsweek*, February 11, pp. 58-63.

Coontz, S. (1992). *The way we never were*. New York: Basic Books.

Coontz, S. (1996). Where are the good old days? *Modern Maturity*, June, pp. 38-43.

Featherstone, J. (1976). *What schools can do*. New York: Liveright.

54% of Children Under 18 Have Working Mothers. (1981). *St. Louis Post-Dispatch*, November 15, p. 16A.

Gergen, K. (1991). *The saturated self*. New York: Basic Books.

Glasser, P. H., & Glasser, L. N. (1970). Adequate family functioning. In P. H. Glasser & L. N. Glasser (Eds.), *Families in crisis*. New York: Harper & Row.

Glick, P. C. (1975). A demographer looks at American families. *Journal of Marriage and the Family, 37* (1), 15-26.

Grand'Maison, J. (1979). The modern family: Locus of resistance or agency of change. In A. Greeley (Ed.), *The family in crisis or in transition*. New York: Seabury Press.

Hall, B. (1995). Families and children first. *Cornell Magazine*, November, pp. 35-41.

Keeney, B. P. (1983). *Aesthetics of change*. New York: Guilford Press.

Lasch, C. (1975). The family and history. *The New York Review of Books*, November 13, pp. 33-37.

Lasch, C. (1979a). *The culture of narcissism*. New York: Warner Books.

Lasch, C. (1979b). *Haven in a heartless world*. New York: Basic Books.

Laslett, B. (1980). Family membership past and present. In A. Skolnick & J. Skolnick (Eds.), *Family in transition*. Boston, MA: Little Brown & Co.

Lazar, I. (1979). Federal policies for families. *Human Ecology Forum, IX* (4), 15-18.

Levi-Strauss, C. (1956). The family. In H. L. Shapiro (Ed.), *Man, culture, and society.* New York: Oxford University Press.

Levitan, S. A., & Belous, (1981). *What's happening to the American family?* Baltimore: MD: Johns Hopkins University Press.

Masnick, G., & Bane, M. J. (1980). *The nation's families:* 1960-1990. Boston, MA: Auburn House.

Maturana, H. R., & Varela, F. J. (1987). *The tree of knowledge.* Boston, MA: New Science Library.

The new baby boom. (1982). *Time,* February 22, pp. 52-58.

Norton, T. M. (1982). Contemporary critical theory and the family: Private world and public crises. In J. B. Elshtain (Ed.), *The family in political thought.* Amherst, MA: The University of Massachusetts Press.

Redfield, J. (1996). *The tenth insight.* New York: Warner Books.

Swerdlow, A., Bridenthal, R., Kelly, J., & Vine, P. (1981). *Household and kin: Families in flux.* Old Westbury, NY: The Feminist Press.

Sullivan, J. (1979). Family support systems paychecks can't buy. *Family Relations, 30* (4), 607-613.

Weigert, A. J., & Hastings, R. (1977). Identity loss, family and social change. *American Journal of Sociology, 82* (6), 1171-1185.

Zimmerman, S. L. (1978). Reassessing the effect of public policy on family functioning. *Social Casework, 59,* 451-457.

Opening Space for Clients' Religious and Spiritual Values in Therapy: A Social Constructionist Perspective

Tim R. Thayne, PhD

SUMMARY. Although spirituality is foundational in many peoples' lives, this dimension is often excluded from therapeutic discussions. This article explores how a social constructionist frame may alleviate the tension created by traditional beliefs concerning spirituality in therapy and foster an open, trusting, climate in which spiritual topics can be discussed. Some of the implications for training therapists in the social constructionist perspective also are considered. *[Article copies available for a fee from The Haworth Document Delivery Service: 1-800-342-9678. E-mail address: getinfo@haworth.com]*

INTRODUCTION

Spiritual strivings and religious beliefs comprise some of the most profound and fertile areas of meaning in people's lives. In fact, Gallop surveys show that 95% of Americans believe in God or a Universal Spirit, and 56% of Americans state that religion is very important in their lives (Payne, Bergin, & Loftus, 1992). Statistics like these make it clear that religion and spirituality can significantly influence people's life orientation and play important supportive roles for them. Clients' spiritual and religious philosophies offer information that is fundamental to how they

---

Tim R. Thayne works and lives in Roanoke, VA.

[Haworth co-indexing entry note]: "Opening Space for Clients' Religious and Spiritual Values in Therapy: A Social Constructionist Perspective." Thayne, Tim R. Co-published simultaneously in *Journal of Family Social Work* (The Haworth Press, Inc.) Vol. 2, No. 4, 1997, pp. 13-23; and: *The Family, Spirituality and Social Work* (ed: Dorothy S. Becvar) The Haworth Press, Inc., 1998, pp. 13-23. Single or multiple copies of this article are available for a fee from The Haworth Document Delivery Service [1-800-342-9678, 9:00 a.m. - 5:00 p.m. (EST). E-mail address: getinfo@haworth.com].

see the world and operate within it. Once this information is gathered, these sacred dimensions of meaning can be utilized as a powerful resource in helping clients deal with the challenges of life.

However, although the spiritual dimension is a valuable resource for many clients, this domain traditionally has been either ignored or discouraged by mental health clinicians. Some of the reasons for this neglect are summarized by Prest and Keller (1993) as follows: (1) the mental health discipline's quest for scientific status invites the profession to distance itself from processes considered subjective and nonscientific; (2) rigid conceptions place spirituality in a deeply personal category that many feel should only be processed with ecclesiastical leaders; and (3) the mental health field's traditional bias links religiosity and spirituality more closely to pathology than to health.

While such barriers are still in force, they are beginning to soften as our awareness of the salience of spirituality for many clients increases. In fact, there is evidence of a counter trend. More and more practitioners and researchers are now exploring how spiritual content can be integrated into a more holistic, collaborative approach to helping clients (Anderson, 1994; Butler & Harper, 1994; Griffith, 1986; Kudlac, 1991; Prest & Keller, 1993; Stander, Piercy, Mackinnon & Helmeke, 1994).

Part of this shift toward more openness to spiritual and religious issues may be due to a developing paradigm within the mental health field, often referred to as postmodernism and the related concepts of a social constructionist epistemology. For postmodern thinkers, true objectivity is unattainable given the perception that the values of the researcher/clinician always have an influence on the process. In regard to research, it is understood that all theoretical constructs, theories of how people change and definitions of pathology and health are influenced by the values of the scientific community from which they originate. From this perspective clinicians also agree that they cannot make a completely objective assessment, nor can they deliver services which are devoid of their own personal values. Understanding that the direction and processes of therapy are strongly influenced by the subjective values of the social worker invites more tolerance and openness to the subjective (i.e., spiritual) values of clients.

At the same time that postmodern influences are changing the way social workers and other practitioners deal with the spiritual realm, scientific studies are painting a picture which indicates that religiosity is not necessarily tied to pathology. In fact, studies are showing quite the opposite. Various beliefs and practices can have a positive, buffering effect on the stresses of personal adjustment, depression, and anxiety when people have an intrinsic orientation toward their religious faith (Bergin, Masters,

& Richards, 1987; Gartner, Larson, & Allen, 1991). This means that they have internalized their beliefs and live them regardless of outside consequences.

However, despite the current trends moving toward more openness, some clinicians may have personal barriers to opening up dialogue on spiritual or religious subjects. They may have different religious or spiritual beliefs than their clients, or may hold to a basically secular orientation and not consider themselves religiously or spiritually oriented. Therefore, they may doubt their ability to relate with clients whose religious values are central to their world view. And even when both the social worker and the client match on religious affiliation, they still may have very different overall world views as their religious beliefs are placed in the context of family background and other cultural variables. Further, social workers may feel uncomfortable entering into a conversation about something as personal as spirituality and religiosity, especially when their own beliefs disagree with those of the client. This is understandable since religious value differences have long been a source of conflict between people.

Although emotional friction may exist, thereby inhibiting individuals from discussing spiritual/religious values, it should not constrain such discussion inside the consulting room. Bergin, Payne, and Richards (1994, p. 21) state that, "Avoiding religious issues or routinely redirecting spiritual concerns in therapy is no more justifiable than refusing to deal with the death of a family member or fears of social encounters." Differences in religious and spiritual beliefs should not keep social workers from entering into an exchange around these relevant topics. Where postmodern thinking has helped the mental health field be more open to accessing the spiritual dimension of client's lives, it also has utility in helping individual clinicians do the same.

In the following sections, the ways in which a postmodern perspective, and specifically that of social constructionism, can enable social workers to open up the therapeutic discussion to the subjective religious/spiritual experiences of their clients in a respectful and helpful way will be considered. Although the definitions of spiritual and religious are different (cf. Ingersoll, 1994), the principles described here apply to both equally well. Therefore, the terms will be used interchangeably throughout. This discussion is preceded by a consideration of the social constructionist perspective which provides the theoretical framework. Some possibilities and cautions in using social constructionist ideas in training new practitioners are addressed in the conclusion.

SOCIAL CONSTRUCTIONISM

Social constructionism is an epistemology which questions the assumptions of the modernist perspective that knowledge can be gained objectively and that it mirrors reality. A postmodern view goes beyond the belief that knowledge may be obtained only through empirical investigation. It sees the knowledge of a group or individual as telling more about the group or culture which possesses it than it does about an ultimate or absolute reality (Paré, 1995).

Social constructionist theorists view knowledge as being created rather than discovered. Current knowledge is dependent upon previous learning, and previous learning takes place in discourse with others, within the context of history and culture. This is to say, our knowledge cannot be free from a construction process, and rather than viewing the construction process as occurring solely as a function of the cognitive processes of individuals (von Glaserfeld, 1984), meaning-making is viewed as happening in the interactional space between people. Meanings evolve into new meanings (Hoffman, 1990) as the social conversations which shape them move forward in time. As Gergen (1985, p. 266) states, " Social constructionism views discourse about the world not as a reflection or map of the world, but as an artifact of communal interchange."

SOCIAL CONSTRUCTIONISM AND SPIRITUALITY IN THERAPY

Clinicians who see meaning and understanding from a social constructionist perspective see clients differently than when looking through the lens of modernism and objectivity. Social constructionism introduces some doubt as to the "reality" of classifications that place behavior in dysfunctional or functional categories. Rather than these classifications coming from objective descriptions of reality, they are seen as the socially constructed assumptions of our culture and of the mental health disciplines. Therefore, if we as clinicians see highly religious people, for example, as pathological, we must realize that such a perspective is founded on the subjective values that we hold.

Accepting this way of thinking about our knowledge, however, does not mean that we need to abandon the guiding standards that promote the well-being of our society. As mental health practitioners, we have the obligation to advance such standards. In other words, we are not promoting anything like "ethical relativism" (Kitchner, 1980) for there are occasions in our clinical work when we must make quick and clear moral judgments (e.g., what to do about child abuse). Rather, we are proposing that we can be more effective when we are hesitant to make value judgments that are isolated from our client's reality. In other words, we must allow the client's construction of his or her religiosity to mold the way we perceive it. Using this approach may be even more important when the world views of the client and the social worker clash, as in the case where there is a difference in religious perspective. In these cases, social constructionism can help us postpone judgment about our client's spiritual experiences while at the same time opening up space for us to understand the complex spiritual meanings they hold. Having a "teachable" attitude then, is one of the benefits of this perspective and may be the most important key in working effectively with clients and their spiritual values.

As social constructionist practitioners, we view ourselves as co-authors (White & Epston, 1990) with the client. This means that we work together in generating meaning that moves the client along toward his or her goals. These new and evolving meanings are brought forth through the medium of language in the context of our discourse with the client.

Co-authoring suggests a joint work whose ideas and meanings are a blend of at least two minds. When the concept of co-authorship is applied to religious meanings, which are the very core aspects of life for many people, we can understand the great vulnerability clients may feel when they are asked to share their religious story. This understanding helps us feel the heavy responsibility that comes with our role in the co-authorship process. To join with the client in creating meaning as personal and foundational as is the spiritual suggests the need to give clients a great amount of agency in leading the discussion, for clients must be the "first author" of their own spiritual story.

Allowing us to co-author such meanings requires an incredible amount of trust on the part of clients. For this reason, our responsibility goes beyond merely informing them of value differences and then proceeding with minimal regard and care for their values. We must allow their stories, and the personal meanings embedded in their stories, to have sway over the way we see them; to truly see the potential for health in their spiritual traditions. Having openness to the good in their belief systems may require us to confront our own stereotypes and prejudices about their particular religious heritage. This, of course, does not mean that we adopt their religious or spiritual beliefs. Rather, we become self-aware of our own biases, while consciously making room to notice and encourage the growth and resources clients' spiritual orientations provide them.

While we are still learning to be led by our client, we may have negative reactions to their religious values. When this happens, it may be important to make them explicit, while at the same time acknowledging that we do not have an objective view point. We must own our feelings and reactions while striving for openness to the meanings our clients hold. After all, if we are truly to join in the authorship process, we must put our name on our ideas and our motivations, making it explicit that they come from our own subjective thinking. By having integrity with our own values, which for me includes esteeming highly the spiritual meanings held by clients, trust and security is created as clients see that their values change us in terms of how we see them. Trust also increases as it becomes apparent to them that their religious values influence the direction of the therapeutic discussion.

When we come from a social constructionist perspective, we are interested in entering into the therapeutic process *together* with our clients. This, to me, goes beyond being merely a co-author of the meanings created in the session. Such togetherness also begins to describe the type of relationship required between clients and ourselves in order to be open to being mutually and reciprocally influenced by each other. More than being honest in terms of informing our clients of our motives, it requires a deeper level of commitment on our part, one that is referred to as *honoring* clients in the relationship. This quality of relating means having genuine respect for their ideas and beliefs, which is prerequisite to entering into a meaningful discussion around issues as significant and personal as spiritual values. Clients feel greater safety in discussing pertinent spiritual issues when such an atmosphere has been fostered.

Honoring religious values also entails recognizing within the conversation the feelings associated with those values. Without empathy for the client's emotional level, the social worker may only approach understanding of the content and completely miss the depth and therefore, the essence of the issue. For example, the social worker who does not open space for honoring of religious values may not understand the deep existential loss a Buddhist grandfather may feel when his grandchild marries a Christian. On the other hand, recognition of such feelings may build the therapeutic alliance and may further demonstrate to the client that the social worker can not only be informed but can understand spiritual concerns.

Such a relationship is not attained by "trying" to create togetherness as a technique, although this is what it may seem is being proposed in traditional modernistic approaches to clinical practice. That is, practitioners are told to value their clients' world-views before going forward with their expert opinion and intervention. Such a request often seems more difficult than performing the human contortions seen at the circus. In other words, how can professionals who see themselves as experts bridle their hypotheses while at the same time fully appreciating clients' beliefs? Indeed, some important elements of the clients' discourse may be lost during the process of wrestling to hold back so-called expert knowledge. Only by giving up the "knowing" position can they be free to assume the "not-knowing" position, which may prove to be far more beneficial to the client (Anderson & Goolishian, 1992).

By holding this not-knowing perspective, we allow clients room to discuss the meanings that are most significant to them. By contrast, professionals practicing under modernist assumptions according to which they see themselves as experts may find it difficult to be coaxed into following conversational trails that do not fit with their theories. The words "coaxed" and "trail" are used because they remind me of a horse I once owned named Pop. From time to time Pop "knew" where he wanted to go and he could not be side-tracked from his goal. Even though I was supposed to be choosing the direction, and seemingly was in the position to do so, he was in control. No amount of coaxing would change his mind. Stubborn horses, who know where they want to go, may be similar to practitioners who think of themselves as experts. Social workers who can be led by the client regarding significant issues become experts in providing space for relevant religious discussions. Being able to be taught and led by the client may be particularly comforting to therapists who lack understanding of particular religious language and meanings. In many ways, being truly ignorant of these issues may help generate the level of curiosity it takes to become informed by the client.

A social constructionist frame places all realities (within certain limits) on a par with one another and in the process undermines the tendency of the clinician to think of him/herself as the expert. Social workers who are working with clients holding different religious values must see clients' values as more central in the therapeutic process than their own values. This will, as Anderson and Goolishian (1992, p. 30) write, "allow clients room for conversational movement and space, since they no longer have to promote, protect, or convince the therapist of their view." There may be a paradoxical lesson here worth noting; it takes much space in order to achieve togetherness.

IMPLICATIONS FOR CLINICAL TRAINING

Many training centers for mental health practitioners are currently involved in helping their students deal with the challenges of diversity. Classes on gender and ethnicity are required in the curriculum. The necessity of grappling with diverse values will only increase as we move forward into the 21st century. Bergin et al. (1994, p. 23), put it well in the following:

> Diversity itself, with all its trouble and divisiveness, may be our best bet to prosper in facing value dilemmas. In facing conflicting and incompatible values, destructive values and consensual values, diversity calls into question one-sidedness or quick and impulsive solutions. Unity may be feasible in broad strokes, adopting general guidelines and mutually beneficial principles, but on specifics there will always be diversity in a free society. Diversity may be the hallmark of freedom and personal agency.

It therefore becomes important to question existing assumptions within the field that may hinder our ability to deal with diversity. Training in many different therapeutic models may help clinicians facilitate work in different value orientations, but education is needed around the epistemological assumptions that are foundational to the different models. This more abstract and philosophical level, whether deliberately taught or not, directs our attention to the assumptions underlying the definitions of pathology and health, the use of values, and how change occurs.

Social constructionism may be an important aspect of the learning process for social workers and other practitioners in training, who might benefit from having a basic understanding of this perspective for the following three reasons. First, social constructionism is gaining momentum in the mental health field (Gergen, 1985) and is foundational to many of the emerging models of practice. Secondly, during a time of such diversity in values, including spiritual beliefs, the call is going out for the need to honor these differing values. Ideas that help students balance issues of general ethics and individual values are being called for in training institutions. Social constructionism seems to be a useful philosophy to consider in light of our need to accommodate such diversity. And thirdly, a social constructionist frame may help increase the practitioner's ability to develop trusting relationships with his or her clients; a factor which has been shown to be most critical in therapeutic outcome.

There are some important cautions, however, for supervisors when using social constructionist ideas in training. Great care should be taken that discussions not slip into ethical relativism. In other words, the belief that reality is constructed may be taken as far as to say that there is no "truth." This is a debate that eventually may evolve toward a debate on the subject of religion and God. Whether the moral laws we hold to as a civilization are socially constructed or are inherent in the way the universe and human beings were created by Deity, it does not seem to matter.

Suffering still occurs as people break those laws (Kitchner, 1980). Social constructionist views should be offered as a philosophy that social workers can take or leave, but one that is often useful. To promote it as more than that, as "truth," would be inconsistent with its very premises. Social constructionism, therefore, becomes a tool for thinking when working with others where there is a need to empathize and understand their position.

For some students, for whom religion is central to their world-view, social constructionism can be accepted as a theory that explains much of our knowledge, but not all of it. They may see it as describing to a great extent the human processes of meaning-making, but not as fitting for all knowledge. For them, religious understandings and spiritual knowledge is transcendent relative to what is normally known, as these are knowledges that are given to humankind through faith; processes different from gaining knowledge through the five senses. In short, practitioners in training may benefit from gaining an education in the social constructionist philosophy when the training does not tyrannize their own ontological belief system.

CONCLUSION

Traditionally, religious and spiritual values have not been topics considered relevant in mental health settings. This belief is beginning to change. There is growing acceptance that the spiritual/theistic values of clients should be honored and utilized in the therapy process, however, there are still barriers to overcome. The first barrier is that religiously-oriented clients have expressed concern over entering counseling with secular social workers, fearing that their own values will not be honored as viable. Second, where differences exist between therapist/client religious values, both may feel hesitant to enter into dialogue around spiritual/theistic issues.

Approaches to social work which use a social constructionist lens may prove helpful in combating both barriers discussed above. Clients who enter therapy with practitioners who hold this philosophy may be more likely to feel comfortable sharing spiritual/religious concerns as an atmosphere of respect and openness is engendered. Social workers with this perspective consider the story given by the client central to any treatment they might offer. They give up the expert position to the client, taking a learning position. Such a stance may increase clients' conversational mobility around religious and spiritual issues.

Differences in values between practitioners and their clients are less a concern since putting on this lens allows for meanings other than one's own to have validity in their given context. In other words, it is not requisite that the client and social worker share the same values in order for the values of the client to be important in this perspective. Thus, training in social constructionist ideas may be a helpful way to prepare for working with clients of diverse values. Care should be taken that ethical relativism is not promoted and that the ontological belief system of the clinician in training be respected.

REFERENCES

Anderson, D. A. (1994). Transcendence and relinquishment in couple therapy. *Journal of Systemic Therapies, 13*, 36-41.

Anderson, H., & Goolishian, H. (1992). The client is the expert: A not-knowing approach to therapy. In S. McNamee, & K. J. Gergen (Eds.), *Therapy as social construction* (pp. 25-39). London: Sage Publications.

Bergin, A. E., Masters, K. S., & Richards, P. S. (1987). Religiousness and mental health reconsidered: A study of an intrinsically religious sample. *Journal of Counseling Psychology, 34*, 197-204.

Bergin, A. E., Payne, I. R. & Richards, P. S. (1994). Values in psychotherapy. Unpublished manuscript, Brigham Young University, Provo, UT.

Butler, M. H., & Harper, J. M. (1994). The divine triangle: God in the marital system of religious couples. *Family Process, 33*, 277-286.

Gartner, J., Larson, D. B., & Allen, G. D. (1991). Religious commitment and mental health: A review of the empirical literature. *Journal of Psychology and Theology, 19*, 6-25.

Gergen, K. J. (1985). The social constructionist movement in modern psychology. *American Psychologist, 40*, 266-275.

Griffith, J. L. (1986). Employing the God-family relationship in therapy with religious families. *Family Process, 25*, 609-618.

Hoffman, L. (1990). Constructing realities: An art of lenses. *Family Process, 29*, 1-12.

Ingersoll, R. E. (1994). Spirituality, religion, and counseling: Dimensions and relationships. *Counseling and Values, 38*, 98-111.

Kitchner, R. F. (1980). Ethical relativism and behavior therapy. *Journal of Consulting and Clinical Psychology, 48*, 1-7.

Kudlac, K. E. (1991). Including God in the conversation: The influence of religious beliefs on the problem-organized system. *Family Therapy, 18*, 277-285.

Payne, R., Bergin, A. E., & Loftus, P. E. (1992). A review of attempts to integrate spiritual and standard psychotherapy techniques. *Journal of Psychotherapy Integration, 2*, 171-192.

Paré, D. A. (1995). Of families and other cultures: The shifting paradigm of family therapy. *Family Process, 34*, 1-19.

Prest, L. A., & Keller, J. F. (1993). Spirituality and family therapy: Spiritual beliefs, myths, and metaphors. *Journal of Marital and Family Therapy, 19,* 137-148.

Stander, V., Piercy, F. P., Mackinnon, D., & Helmeke, K. (1994). Spirituality, religion and family therapy: Competing or complementary worlds? *The American Journal of Family Therapy, 22,* 27-41.

von Glaserfeld, C. (1984). An introduction to radical constructivism. In P. Waltzlawick (Ed.), *The invented reality* (pp. 17-40), New York: Norton.

White, M., & Epston, D. (1990). *Narrative means to therapeutic ends.* New York: W. W. Norton.

Addressing Spiritual/Religious Issues in Therapy: Potential Problems and Complications

Milo F. Benningfield, PhD

SUMMARY. Recent years have seen a strong interest on the part of mainstream mental health professionals in clients' religious/spiritual concerns. Several phenomena have contributed to this interest and encouraged psychotherapists to address such concerns in therapy. However, the therapist's own personal biases, lack of adequate education, personal discomfort and self-serving needs can contribute to problems and complications in therapy when addressing religious/ spiritual issues, ten of which are described and discussed in this article. *[Article copies available for a fee from The Haworth Document Delivery Service: 1-800-342-9678. E-mail address: getinfo@haworth.com]*

INTRODUCTION

A spiritual life of some kind is absolutely necessary for psychological "health"; at the same time, excessive or ungrounded spirituality can also be dangerous, leading to all kinds of compulsive and even violent behavior. (Moore, 1992)

Recent years have seen the emergence of interest among mainstream psychotherapists in the issue of religion/spirituality.[1] Previously, however,

---

Milo F. Benningfield is in private practice, Dallas, TX.

[Haworth co-indexing entry note]: "Addressing Spiritual/Religious Issues in Therapy: Potential Problems and Complications." Benningfield, Milo F. Co-published simultaneously in *Journal of Family Social Work* (The Haworth Press, Inc.) Vol. 2, No. 4, 1997, pp. 25-42; and: *The Family, Spirituality and Social Work* (ed: Dorothy S. Becvar) The Haworth Press, Inc., 1998, pp. 25-42. Single or multiple copies of this article are available for a fee from The Haworth Document Delivery Service [1-800-342-9678, 9:00 a.m. - 5:00 p.m. (EST). E-mail address: getinfo@haworth.com].

25

there was little appreciation for any aspect of the integration of spirituality and psychotherapy in the professional literature. And the literature which did exist emphasized the integration of the two primarily through anecdotal material and personal vignettes.

At least four phenomena have contributed to the surge of interest among traditional mental health professionals in spiritual aspects of the client's life. First is the flourishing of the alternative, or complementary, medicine movement. Increasing numbers of Americans have become dissatisfied with a pathology model of medicine that limits intervention to a specific or narrow focus on a problem or procedure. The alternative medicine field takes a more holistic approach to the person, emphasizing body, mind, and spirit. Dean Ornish, a Harvard trained cardiologist, recently stunned his colleagues with pictures of angiograms demonstrating that life-style changes can actually open up clogged arteries. He states, "I'm increasingly convinced that we are dealing here with emotional and spiritual dimensions" (Wallis, 1991, p. 75).

Second, writings by respected psychotherapy practitioners and researchers in the mental health field have provided information regarding significant connections between spirituality and psychotherapy. The purchase of more than three million copies of physician Scott Peck's book, *The Road Less Traveled* (1978) attests to the growing interest in the relationship between spirituality and psychotherapy. More recently, two other books by well respected authors have informed clinicians on this topic. Lovinger's (1984) *Working With Religious Issues in Therapy* is a kind of instruction guide for psychotherapists to help them become informed and skilled at addressing religious issues with their clients. Spero's (1985) edited book, *Psychotherapy of the Religious Patient,* examines a variety of technical and ethical problems encountered by the therapist who addresses religious issues with clients.

A third influence pertaining to the relationship between spirituality and psychotherapy is the self-help group movement. The 1980s witnessed an explosion of self-help groups promoting an informal spirituality in 12-step programs that encouraged members to surrender to a "higher power." Thousands of individuals who never previously had an interest in organized religion or who had rejected their childhood faith began embracing this simple recipe for psychological and spiritual growth. Large numbers of those same individuals began entering psychotherapy, describing how this new religion was changing their lives. Thus, therapists were required to learn about the spiritual beliefs of their clients and to be conversant about spiritual subjects in order to communicate with them (Butler, 1990).

Fourth, there has been a growing interest in Eastern philosophies, with their emphasis on the health of the individual, attracting both the lay public and the mental health community. Millions of people have been drawn to Eastern philosophy's emphasis on the transcendent or spiritual aspects of life and its influence on one's psychological health (Moyers, 1993).

Unfortunately, however, the majority of psychotherapists are ill-prepared to work with the spiritual dimension of their clients' lives. Although increasing numbers of professional training programs and supervision experiences have begun to address other issues in the client/therapist relationship such as racial, gender, and ethnic concerns, little attention is given to the client/therapist connection pertaining to spiritual issues. The current state of the mental health field is such that despite increasing awareness of the relevance of religious/spiritual issues, there are few training experiences, educational programs or supervision opportunities available which include such a focus.

Regardless of the shortage of formal training in dealing with these issues, increasing numbers of psychotherapists are facing them in their consulting rooms. And the therapist's views about spirituality can be both an asset and a potential obstacle in the therapeutic process (Prest & Keller, 1993). Even those mental health practitioners who have expertise in this area of engagement are not immune to the perils and pitfalls that may emerge when attempting to integrate spirituality and psychotherapy. Thus, while there has been increasing support for such an integration within the psychotherapy field, others have a concern about the appropriateness of this development. They emphasize the need to be aware of potential problems associated with the introduction of spiritual and religious issues into traditional psychotherapy practice (Younggren, 1993).

It is the author's belief that psychotherapists, with the proper education and training experiences, can effectively help clients address religious and spiritual issues in the context of therapy. With greater experience, it is hoped that we all will learn to achieve a better balance in navigating this largely uncharted realm of the client's growth and healing process. Until then, we must settle for the small amount of data we have from personal experience and the few published examples from other clinicians. The following is an attempt to summarize this data into 10 areas about which it is important to be aware, using case examples as illustration wherever possible.

ATTEMPTED NEUTRALITY

Being neutral or unbiased is generally considered a virtue for which psychotherapists should strive. That is, psychotherapy is founded on the admonition to be objective, detached, non-judgmental, and morally neutral. Trainees are encouraged to go to great lengths not to impose their personal values, beliefs, or morals on their clients. However, as more experienced professionals know, it is virtually impossible to be completely neutral in therapeutic work with others. If one is passionate about one's work, if one desires to facilitate the growth and health of those with whom one works, then it is impossible to be neutral or value-free in dealing with one's clients. We value health over ill-health, emotional fitness over emotional emptiness, personal autonomy over domination, assertive independence over fearful dependence.

As with most therapeutic issues, however, there is not unanimous agreement on this point. Frankl (1984), for example, believes that one's moral and ethical convictions are powerful resources with clients and should be used without apology in the therapeutic process. On the other hand, Albert Ellis (1962; 1983) adamantly opposes the notion that one's personal values should have any place in the consultation room. Whether the therapist thinks that he or she should use moral and ethical convictions without apology or attempt to banish them from the therapy session, the fact remains that the therapist's beliefs, values, and morals do play a part in his or her work with clients.

Perhaps the most responsible approach the psychotherapist can take on the issue is to be aware that he or she cannot be completely neutral with clients. Furthermore, therapists need to recognize that their ignorance of this fact can have negative consequences for clients and the therapeutic process. Lovinger's (1979) concept of a value-neutral approach with clients appears to be a balanced approach to this issue.

Case Example

Mrs. Johnson called Dr. Kent to inquire about marital therapy. She said that he had been highly recommended to her and her husband as a marital therapist. She also explained that it was very important that their therapist be sympathetic to their strong Evangelical faith and practices. Dr. Kent responded that he could be trusted to be sympathetic to the couple's religious beliefs and practices. In the second session Mrs. Johnson proclaimed that her husband was more open and expressive with Dr. Kent than with any of the other therapists they had seen, and that her husband's attitudes were having a positive impact on the marital relationship. Mr. Johnson nervously laughed in agreement. The third session focused on a fight the couple had during the previous week and addressed conflict management. When they left, they appeared to be satisfied with the results of the session. However, Mrs. Johnson called two days later and canceled the fourth scheduled session along with all additional sessions. When Dr.

Kent sought an explanation for the decision to terminate therapy, Mrs. Johnson explained that when the couple attempted to get Dr. Kent to share his religious beliefs about Christian couples fighting, they felt he was guarded and evasive in his responses. She went on to say that although Dr. Kent had said in the initial telephone conversation that he could be sympathetic to their religious convictions, it was obvious from the many statues and carvings of Indian medicine men, shamans, and other healers besides Christ which decorated his office that he was far "too liberal" in his views for them.

Obviously, there is the possibility that there was nothing that Dr. Kent could have done or said to make the couple comfortable enough to continue working with him effectively. On the other hand, if Dr. Kent had spent more time "hearing out" this couples' need to be reassured that he could understand and appreciate their religious concerns and if he had been willing to talk more frankly about his own religious views in a professional manner, it is also possible that they might have been able to continue working with him productively.

It is important to remember that no one can act out of exclusively pure or neutral motives. Even the noblest deeds are based on a mixture of pure and impure motivations. The wise psychotherapist acknowledges this dilemma. Knowing and accepting this fact is a first step in understanding and dealing with the challenges involved when addressing spiritual/religious issues with clients.

INACCURATE OR INCOMPLETE DIAGNOSIS

Mainstream mental health practitioners are trained to do diagnostic evaluations of clients regarding emotional and mental functioning and to assess in detail clients' family backgrounds and environmental stressors. However, not only do they receive little or no training in how to assess a client's religious or spiritual values, but also they lack training in determining ways these values influence the client's past or current functioning or how they may influence the therapy process. If therapists are to be effective in assisting clients with spiritual/religious concerns, they must know how to conduct an evaluation of this aspect of the client's life. Psychiatrist and theologian Elizabeth Bowman (1987) notes that as mental health professionals we would not think of beginning therapy with a client on any subject without first obtaining background information concerning the client's experiences in that area. Similarly, she points out, one should not attempt to work with religious issues before obtaining a religious history.

Case Example

Misdiagnosis of religious influences appears to have contributed to the therapist's inability to help the couple more effectively in a case described by Ilda Ficher and J. D. Kaplan (1985), two experienced psychotherapists. At first glance it appeared to be a simple case of unconsummated marriage that would respond effectively to sex therapy. The couple were intelligent, well-educated, and cooperative. The wife, a school counselor, and the husband, a physical therapist, had been married seven years without ever having sexual intercourse. Following some individual and conjoint sessions the couple discontinued therapy for a month's vacation and never returned for additional consultation. In a follow-up telephone call it was revealed that the sexual problem had not changed and the couple did not believe additional sex therapy would benefit them.

In analyzing her failure with this couple, Dr. Ficher stated that it was "directly related to an error in the original assessment of the couple" (1985, p. 209). What had not been adequately assessed were the powerful religious issues. The wife had been reared in a religious Catholic home and had strongly internalized religious values. She perceived priests as more mature and wiser and better as persons than other people, and thus attributed the sexual problem to herself.

Her husband, a former priest, had entered the priesthood to fulfill his mother's wishes, while rejecting his father's wishes for him to become a physician. Thus, his impotence reflected his conflict of vocation, "forever half priest and half not, rebelling against his natural father and his spiritual father, but never going all the way" (1985, p. 218). One sees in this example that even highly trained and highly skilled therapists can fail with clients when religious values and issues are minimized or inadequately assessed.

MISUSE OF POWER

Effective psychotherapists are powerful individuals. Their power is experienced by their clients, who are often drawn to it inexorably. This is true whether one is dealing with secular issues or spiritual concerns. The early medicine man and his power were related to the fact that he was not only a doctor but also a priest in contact with higher forces. The therapist's power is double-edged. It can add greatly to the client's personal growth and development. The same power also can severely hurt and damage the client. Long the case, the history of healing reveals that among those who were assumed to be in direct contact with the gods were some who misused their power.

Psychotherapists, even today, are not immune from such misuses. Operating outside the boundaries of self-restraint, some therapists at times place their own needs first and violate the purpose for the relationship: service to the client. This lack of adherence to their own professional values and to the commitment to clients disrupts or destroys the connection between therapist and client. Peterson (1992), writing on the professional's struggle with power, explains that many have difficulty with the concept and some are even frightened by it. She quotes a therapist as saying: "Getting in touch with my power scared me because I realized what kind of impact I could have. I could be ruthless with my power. I got frightened because it didn't fit with who I thought I was. I didn't want to own my dark side. I would like to pretend I'm not that powerful" (1992, p. 52).

Case Example

Bob and Jan sought help with their marital communication. They were referred by their pastor to a particular psychologist because he regularly worked with couples' religious concerns and conflicts. After seeing the couple in four conjoint sessions, the therapist recommended individual therapy for Jan, to whom he had become attracted. He explained to the couple that he believed that once Jan worked through some of her confusion regarding religious matters that marital sessions with Bob and Jan together could then be entered into more productively. The psychologist saw Jan for three months in individual therapy before she discontinued with him altogether and the couple sought help elsewhere.

Jan explained to their next therapist that the psychologist would give her assignments consisting of scripture reading dealing with marriage and the family. When she attempted to discuss current marital difficulties, he reportedly gave her scripture readings pertaining to those issues and recommended they discuss the scripture readings at the next session. Jan experienced the therapist as having a strong need to have her listen to him and compliment him on his Biblical knowledge and expertise. When he began commenting on her attractive appearance with uncomfortable frequency, she felt she was meeting his needs rather than having her own needs addressed.

In this instance, the therapist was using his position of power and influence to structure the therapy sessions to meet his needs rather than those of the clients. He took advantage of the client's religious struggles and trust in him as a spiritual and psychological guide.

SEXUAL MISCONDUCT

Taking advantage of clients sexually probably has occurred from the earliest of times (Bates & Brodsky, 1989.) We would like to think that those therapists who sexually abuse clients are sick, ill-trained, insensitive, and incompetent as practitioners. Often, however, that is not the case. Rutter (1986, p. 8), writing about one of his special mentors, says:

> I was one among many younger therapists, both men and women, who considered him a uniquely valuable role model, that special kind of teacher who inspires both outer and inner development. On the outer, practical level he taught us specific skills of psychotherapy; on the inner level he helped awaken in us a personal sense of ethical and creative involvement with our work. He was a man who articulated for the rest of us the most humane values of our profession.

Rutter (1986) later learned that his mentor frequently engaged in sexual relations with many of his female patients.

It is well known that mental health practitioners can become infatuated with their patients or clients and be vulnerable to the expression of their sexual desires in the professional relationship. Many mental health professionals still seem to believe that such infatuations or vulnerabilities are unlikely to surface when the focus of therapy is on addressing religious or spiritual issues with clients. However, those who attend regularly to the spiritual dimensions of clients' lives are not immune to overstepping the sexual boundary with patients. Psychotherapist Jack Kornfield (1993, p. 254) states, "I have encountered many students who were painfully affected by the misdeeds of their teachers. I have heard such stories about . . . Christian priests, nuns and everybody in between."

Addressing spiritual/religious concerns can have a powerful effect on clients, stimulating all manner of emotions and sensations, including sexual. May, a psychiatrist working with spiritual directors, observes that some of those helping persons have, for their own sexual desires, exploited individuals whom they are commissioned to help. He says that it has long been known that "spiritual awakening and growth" (1992, p. 136) gives rise to sexual feelings, as defenses are lessened and psychological blocks are removed.

Similarly, psychotherapists who regularly work with clinical hypnosis are acutely aware that strong erotic feelings can be generated on the part of the client when the latter is in an altered mental state. In a presentation to psychotherapists on cautions in the use of hypnosis, Wall (1992) described a case in which a psychologist took great care to introduce hypnosis to a client slowly and responsibly. Nevertheless, following the first hypnosis session, the woman said that upon becoming fully hypnotized, "I had the experience of you making wonderful, passionate love to me!"

Obviously, the eliciting of sexual feelings is not automatically a negative event in the therapeutic encounter. In fact, it is often expected in order to help accomplish the client's goals of understanding and coping with personal problems in the sexual area. In some circumstances, if spiritual issues are not addressed, blocked affect may never become available— sexual or otherwise. Therapists who ignore or minimize the degree to which sexual or erotic feelings can be elicited in therapy, both in themselves and in their clients, may make themselves unnecessarily vulnerable to sexual impropriety.

Case Example

Charles, a marital therapist in private practice, confided while consulting with a colleague on some cases that he had not been satisfied in his marriage for some time, especially sexually. He went on to say that he was beginning to find pleasure in "seeing if I can elicit interest in me from some of my attractive female patients." He also described a reluctance to recommend marital therapy with some couples in which he found the wife attractive and fantasized seeing her in individual sessions. The son of a minister, Charles divulged that when he was able to engage women in discussions "around religious or spiritual concerns, it seems to enable me to get close to them more quickly."

Charles not only was attempting to awaken a sexual desire in some of his female clients, but also to use their religious/spiritual concerns to increase their vulnerability to his own personal needs. "It is one of the oldest charlatan tricks to try to bind women patients by awakening sexual desire. It is very easy for a psychotherapist to fall into this particular aspect," declares Guggenbuhl-Craig (1982, p. 39).

INADEQUATE LIMIT-SETTING

Limit-setting is important in all forms of psychotherapy and is taught in all accredited mental health training programs. But working with spiritual or religious issues seems to pose special challenges for some therapists. Several years ago the author noted that many clergy and pastoral counselors had difficulty setting time-limits in their counseling sessions (Benningfield, 1969). While thoughtful flexibility is required with all clients, it is inappropriate to gratify clients' demands for religious or spiritual discussions, religious readings, and so on at the expense of addressing important psychological or emotional problems.

Some therapists find themselves so fascinated and over-invested with a client's experiences in a particular aspect of their lives that they become stuck along with the client. At times, for example, a therapist may become so invested in providing corrective spiritual experiences for those clients with a history of religious or spiritual deprivation that the client's other important non-spiritual needs are neglected. Thus the therapist may inadvertently collude with the client's desire not to get into uncomfortable psychological issues by deflecting conversation onto religious or spiritual matters. By becoming over-protective and too non-directive, the therapist may not allow the client to experience painful feelings of hurt, anxiety, or guilt which may need to be experienced and worked through.

Case Example

Robert had been a school counselor for several years and was receiving training and supervision in marital and family therapy. He had also recently returned to a church community, after having rejected that aspect of his life for several years. Finding much satisfaction and excitement in the study of the Bible and other religious literature, he would eagerly share his renewed faith and Biblical discoveries with his supervisor and colleagues at every opportunity. Robert began to do this with his clients as well. He found himself particularly drawn to clients who were struggling with spiritual issues or to those, like himself, who were making new discoveries in this particular area of their lives. Thus, it was not uncommon for Robert to elicit from clients various religious or spiritual concerns and engage in stimulating dialogue with them around those issues.

Working with clients' issues in the spiritual realm did not create a problem for Robert or his clients. Indeed, he worked with them in this part of their lives productively. The problem that arose for him was in the area of time management. While very systematic and time-conscious in most areas of his therapy work, Robert seemed to lose all sense of time when addressing spiritual issues with clients. He would "hate to cut someone off when they are in the middle of reading an important Biblical passage or just when they are explaining some new insight about their faith." With some of his clients he would conclude the session with prayer, initiating it himself or permitting them to do so. However, it was not uncommon for these prayers to run well into another client's therapy time.

COUNTERTRANSFERENCE

When a client demonstrates difficult resistances, acts out internal conflict, or presents material that is difficult to hear, therapists may tend to withdraw from an optimal therapeutic stance and become over-identified or under-identified with the client. According to Bowman (1989), the most common source of therapist error is related to countertransference concerning religion. Whether the view of religion is a positive, encouraging one or a negative, rejecting one, religious issues are likely to cause problems for the therapist. While the same might be said of any value or conviction held by the therapist, it may be that the spiritual is less conscious and thus more affect-laden than other values. For example, unresolved negative feelings from childhood or adolescence may interfere with the therapist's ability to be objective enough to assist a client in working through his or her negative or frustrated feelings toward Deity. Therapists who have unfinished business with their religious beliefs are at risk of using therapy as a vehicle for acting out hostile impulses harbored against their parents and religious traditions (Spero, 1985).

Positive countertransference of religion or spiritual material can be problematic as well. The therapist may become so fascinated or interested in the philosophy or theological content of the client's spiritual beliefs or journey that he or she loses sight of the psychological dynamic significance of the data. Or the therapist may share the client's position that spiritual or religious material is sacrosanct and therefore not subject to the kind of critical examination that other subjects receive in psychotherapy. "This results," states Bowman, "in an inability to recognize the wolf of resistance beneath the sheep's clothing of religious ideation" (1989, p. 544).

Case Example

A 17-year-old religious Jewish man was being seen by a psychologist who belonged to the same religious community as the client. Arriving at his initial session agitated, the client let the therapist know that all the secular psychologists he had seen had failed to appreciate the importance of religion in his life. At the same time, he complained that all the religious counselors he had encountered failed to appreciate the depth of his psychological struggles.

With permission from the client, the therapist communicated with their mutual rabbi, a former religion teacher of the therapist (who was currently the teacher of the client), as well as the client's grandparents. The rationale was that each was in a position to offer important psychological perspectives on the client. The contacts were a mistake. The therapist actually had keen insight into the client's need for individuality and independence in relation to the religious and family aspects of his life. However, the therapist's own unresolved issues in those areas, and his need to be seen by his rabbi and former religion teacher as expert with both the client's religious and psychological difficulties, interfered with his ability to stay focused on the needs of the client. After three episodes in which the client abruptly left therapy and then returned as a way of reacting to the psychologist's countertransference issues, which the psychologist failed to address, the client finally terminated therapy, to the relief of both (Spero, 1985).

DISCOMFORT WITH RELIGIOUS/SPIRITUAL MATERIAL

No matter how well-trained or experienced a therapist may be, there are areas of practice with which he or she is uncomfortable. For some, it is the area of religion/spirituality. The discomfort may result simply from experiencing little exposure to this dimension of life while growing up. It may be related to unresolved negative experiences with a spiritual person, community, or religious tradition. Or it could be related to the therapist's anxiety regarding fundamental questions of humankind such as life and death, good and evil, suffering and health. In an effort to avoid these issues in his or her own life, the therapist may discourage their introduction into the therapy hour.

There are many subtle but effective ways the therapist can discourage the elaboration of spiritual material in therapy. These include lifting an eyebrow at the introduction of spiritual issues; treating them as indicators of neurotic, immature facets of the client; and representing a pathological problem (Butler, 1990).

Case Example

A former client wrote to a therapist when she discovered the therapist's interest in the integration of spirituality into her work:

> Bravo! Your interest in helping clients explore spiritual issues is super! I've experienced that uncomfortable silence and avoidance of the subject during sessions with my former therapists. It was a little bewildering to feel that such *important* parts of my life were not important enough to explore. What a blessing it would be to discuss them openly–without feeling like you're making your therapist squirm.

THERAPIST ARROGANCE

People turn to psychotherapists today the way they once turned to the Greek oracles, the shaman, or members of the clergy. Mistrusting their own inner voice and lacking a sense of direction or purpose, clients look to gurus for guidance and endow those persons with wisdom and power. This can become very intoxicating to the therapist and may lead to a false sense of importance and omniscience. Herron and Rouslin (1984) believe that a principal hazard of the profession of psychotherapy is the belief that we really are special. Clients usually choose us but we generally run the program. We choose what will be talked about, how it will be interpreted, and what actions should be taken. The problem is not that we can make a positive difference in the client's life, but in forgetting that we are not the wise all-knowing persons we would like to be.

Restraining our egos is a challenge many of us will never quite overcome, according to Kottler (1986). With all our education, consulting contracts, licenses, and busy schedules supervising others, it is hard not to take ourselves seriously and believe our pronouncements to be profound. Typically, therapists tend to ignore spiritual issues and have their own rationale for that which they believe makes them authoritative.

Some psychotherapists who do or do not identify strongly with a particular spiritual path or religious orientation nevertheless feel obligated to counsel from that particular belief or lack of belief. They may even hold that they genuinely do have the correct approach to clients' problems. However, such a posture, no matter how well-intended, encourages a prejudicial, judgmental stance that is antithetical to the type of openness and receptivity that fosters personal and relationship growth.

On the opposite side is the stance of Richard Patterson, a clinical psychologist who specializes in family therapy and has a sensitivity to clients' religious and spiritual issues. In speaking candidly about himself, Patterson confides, "I wish I could claim to be free of judgment . . . [but] I find judgment creeping into my thoughts and into my words" (1992, p. 37).

The beginning of therapy is often like a parent-child relationship with the therapist in the position of knowing and the client in a regressed state of neediness. Guggenbuhl-Craig (1982) observes that psychotherapists are often forced into a position of omniscience by clients and are expected to know more about ultimate matters, including the transcendent and the spiritual, than does the common person.

The client, therefore, frequently looks to the therapist not only for effective help with immediate problems and concerns, but also for "access to secret knowledge which will enable him to solve all of life's problems" (Guggenbuhl-Craig, 1982, p. 38). Such hopes and expectations can encourage the therapist to imagine himself or herself as special, with special power and knowledge for directing the client's life. It encourages fantasies that he or she is indeed the best and most knowledgeable of healers, the repository of what is needed for the client.

Such therapists may have little difficulty letting clients know that religion or spiritual strivings are a waste of time, a neurotic endeavor of harmful consequence. If the psychotherapist is convinced that his or her faith or spiritual path is the correct one, he or she may not hesitate in telling the client to follow in that direction (Guggenbuhl-Craig, 1982).

The medicine men of old, the archaic healers, were always regarded as powerful persons who resorted to any means in order to retain their status. However, just as the temptation of the teacher is to arrogance, the temptation of the client is to subservience and dependency. The client's desire to find and surrender to the perfect parent, the one who at least points one in the right direction, can be very exhilarating to the therapist and encourage her or him to think more highly of self than is appropriate (Guggenbuhl-Craig, 1982).

Case Example

Robert is an intelligent, articulate, charming 46-year-old psychologist. In his graduate school program he was class president and later while in private practice served on the licensing board of his state psychological association. He greatly enjoys his work, viewing himself as an exceptional psychotherapist. He has strong ideas about what is best for his patients and is quick to let them and colleagues know his opinions. Some of his colleagues–including his wife–complain that he is a bit too cocky and opinionated.

Robert's patients seem to respect him and benefit from their work with him. Thus, it was quite a shock when he told a trusted colleague that he had been sexually involved with three of his female patients, two married and one single. When questioned about this behavior, he stated matter-of-factly that they wanted desperately to have sex with him and that it had proved to be beneficial in each case. All were described as "shut down sexually" and in need of help to "reclaim their sexual libido" and "sense of self-worth." Robert explained that these sexual encounters had occurred several years ago and that he would not think of engaging in such behavior with patients now because of the litigious times in which we live. However, it was apparent to the colleague that Robert thought he was the answer for some of his sexually frustrated female patients in spite of current knowledge and convention regarding therapist-patient sex.

FAILURE TO REALIZE THE BENEFITS
OF RELIGIOUS/SPIRITUAL DIMENSIONS OF LIFE

Many psychotherapists believe that religious or spiritual beliefs or practices play a small, insignificant part in a client's day-to-day living and thus have little to contribute, either positively or negatively, to the psychotherapy process. According to Meyers (1990), they frequently lack awareness of religion and the role it can play in influencing psychological issues. He warns that the failure to consider religious issues may be a serious omission with clients.

The vacuum such an approach creates has been described by Thesenga (1990). During one period in her life she was involved in individual psychotherapy with a therapist who chose not to address her spiritual self. As she reports the situation:

> One half of the raft was my therapy and the other was my spiritual practice. In my psychological work, I was learning more about the complex layers of my personality including my unconscious motivations and buried negativity, but my essential spiritual nature was denied. (1990, p. 78)

Case Example

A 39-year-old woman reported her experience of being in a peer support group with several female therapists. On one occasion she was distraught, feeling that life was passing her by and that she was not contributing anything worthwhile. All but one of her peers encouraged her to find the roots of her frustration in childhood abuse by her alcoholic father. However, it was when one of the group members encouraged her to talk about the need to be fulfilling a purpose, especially one which had an altruistic thrust, that the woman responded with tears and gratitude for being understood.

LACK OF EDUCATION AND TRAINING

Closely related to the psychotherapist's lack of understanding of the significance of spiritual or religious issues to the therapy endeavor is the lack of education and training related to this dimension. Feifel (1958), writing to psychotherapists almost 40 years ago, explained that regardless of our own religious or non-religious beliefs and attitudes, it is important to understand and accept the client's religious position as a significant part of that person's life. Indeed, the religious ideas and beliefs of the client contain material that is most useful to therapy if adequately understood.

However, traditional education in psychology, social work, psychiatry, and family therapy offers little in the area of religion or spirituality. Lovinger (1984) explains that religious traditions are frequently seen as incompatible with the sciences and humanities in several respects. One, the religious assertion of spiritual factors collides with the scientific emphasis on the verification of directly or indirectly observable spirituality and science. Second, the emphasis on belief and faith is inconsistent with the scientific emphasis on curiosity and questioning. And, the intuitive, non-rational aspects of data in spirituality clash with the conventional scientific culture of rational procedures taught in academic programs.

Some therapists are quite aware that they are lacking in the subjects of religion and spirituality and understandably shy away from entering into a client's spiritual life. Clearly, there are several areas in which the therapist should have training and experience in order to deal effectively with the spiritual issues of clients. Being able to distinguish normal needs of spirituality from neurotic ones is imperative. Knowing what type of religious persons the therapist may have difficulties working with can diminish countertransference possibilities. The therapist needs to be clear about his or her own spiritual issues that are not addressed or remain unresolved so that they do not contaminate the treatment needs of the client. The clinician needs to know how a client's religious loyalties, religious community involvement, prayer, and ritual can be helpful resources in psychotherapy. Indeed, it could be considered unethical to ignore a client's spiritual needs when such action could impede the goal toward which the client is working, or, when a failure to understand this dimension of the client's life contributes to a misdiagnosis, and so on. Just as it is important for the psychotherapist to remain current in her and his professional development in the traditional areas of psychotherapy, it behooves him or her to become qualified to address religious/spiritual aspects of the client's life.

CONCLUSION

There are numerous issues of which a therapist must be aware when dealing with clients' spiritual/religious concerns. However, the 10 specific problem areas discussed above can be conceptualized as fitting into two general categories: (1) dealing with the subject inappropriately; and (2) inappropriately avoiding the subject.

These same problem areas obviously can reveal themselves when a therapist is dealing with any issue. For example, if ethnic origin is an important factor, the therapist can mishandle that with inaccurate diagnosis, by therapist arrogance, or by acting out sexually. If the critical issue is the socioeconomic status of a family, the therapist could misdiagnose, attempt neutrality regarding the issue, or even avoid limit setting if the client wished to focus on the personal finances of the therapist.

However, there is one factor which increases the potential for problems and complications in the area of spirituality and religion. That factor is the omission of these subject matters from the professional education of the therapist, both in graduate school and in continuing education offerings. In general, there are two basic antidotes designed to build competence and objectivity and to protect clients from therapist errors. The first is that professionals are inculcated with knowledge and trained in skills pertinent to their profession. Second, they are strongly encouraged to obtain personal therapy and growth experiences which are designed to minimize their unhealthy tendencies and maximize their ability to access their assets. Until very recently, mainstream psychotherapists received neither of these forms of education on the subject of spirituality/religion in their professional graduate education. Even now it is the rare offering. Therapists are not educated and trained in relation to spirituality, nor are they given opportunities to process their own spiritual journeys. Therefore, they are more uneducated, unaware of, and thus more vulnerable to making the errors discussed.

The groundswell of interest is beginning to reach educators and other leaders in the mental health field. When more attention is given to the issue of spirituality in psychotherapy training at all levels, practitioners will be less likely to err either by omission or commission regarding spirituality/religion with their clients. Instead, they will be better prepared to help clients understand and capitalize on this powerful healing resource.

NOTE

1. In this article no distinction is made between client or therapist issues as they pertain to spiritual phenomena, religious beliefs, or values derived from one's personal beliefs or spiritual experience. In addition, the term psychotherapist is used throughout to refer to social workers and other mental health professionals.

REFERENCES

Bates, C. M., & Brodsky, A. M. (1989). *Sex in the therapy hour: A case of professional incest.* New York: Guilford Press.

Benningfield, M. F. (1969). The time factor in multiple-interviewing counseling. *Pastoral Psychology, 20,* 20-28.

Bowman, E. S. (1989). Religious psychodynamics in multiple personality: Suggestions For treatment. *American Journal of Psychotherapy, 41,* 542-553.

Butler, K. (1990). Spirituality reconsidered. *The Family Therapy Networker,* September/October, pp. 26-37.

Ellis, A. (1962). The case against religion: A psychotherapist's view. *The Independent, 126*, 8-16.

Feifel, H. (1958). Introduction to the symposium on the relationship between religion and mental health. *American Psychologist, 13*, 565-566.

Ficher, I., & Kaplan, J. D. (1985). A conflict of vows: The unconsummated marriage of an ex-priest. In S. Coleman (Ed.), *Failures in family therapy* (pp. 208-221). New York: Guilford Press.

Frankl, V. (1984). *Man's search for meaning*. New York: Washington Square Press.

Guggenbuhl-Craig, A. (1982). *Power in the helping professions*. Dallas: Spring Publications.

Herron, R., & Rouslin, B. (1984). The psychotherapist's role in treatment. *Psychotherapy, 35*, 425-431.

Kottler, J. A. (1986). *On becoming a therapist*. San Francisco: Jossey-Bass.

Kornfield, J. (1993). *A path with heart*. New York: Bantam Books.

Lovinger, R. J. (1979). Therapeutic strategies with religious resistances. *Psychotherapy: Theory, Research and Practice, 16*, 419-427.

Lovinger, R. J. (1984). *Working with religious issues in therapy*. New York: Jason Aronson.

May, G. G. (1992). *Care of mind/care of spirit: A psychiatrist explores spiritual direction*. San Francisco: Harper.

Meyers, R. C. (1990). Religious issues in psychotherapy. *Psychotherapy, 24*, 246-253.

Moore, T. (1992). *Care of the soul*. New York: HarperCollins.

Moyers, B. (1993). *Healing and the mind*. New York: Doubleday.

Patterson, R. (1992). *Encounter with angels: Psyche and spirit in the counseling situation*. Chicago: Loyola University Press.

Peck, M. S. (1978). *The road less traveled: A new psychology of life, traditional values, and spiritual growth*. New York: Simon & Schuster.

Peterson, M. R. (1992). *At personal risk: Boundary violations in professional-client relationships*. New York: Norton.

Prest, L., & Keller, J. (1993). Spirituality and family therapy: Spiritual beliefs, myths, and metaphors. *Journal of Marital and Family Therapy, 19*, 137-148.

Rutter, P. (1986). *Sex in the forbidden zone*. Los Angeles: Jeremy P. Tarcher.

Spero, M. H. (Ed.) (1985). *Psychotherapy of the religious patient*. Springfield, IL: Charles C Thomas.

Thesenga, S. (1990, Summer). Spiritual teachers, psychotherapists, and other gurus. *Voices*, pp. 74-80.

Wall, T. (1992). Ethical issues in hypnosis. Workshop for Dallas Society of Clinical Hypnosis, Dallas, Texas.

Wallis, C. (1991). Why new age medicine is catching on. *Time*, November 4, p. 75.

Younggren, J. N. (1993). Ethical issues in religious psychotherapy. *Register Report, 19*, pp. 1-8.

Women's Spirituality:
A Proposed Practice Model

Joyce Hickson, PhD
Andrea Phelps, MS

SUMMARY. The values and spirituality of clients are an important area for social workers, counselors, and other mental health professionals to consider in their work. This article addresses the need for professionals to be sensitive to this aspect of growth and development for all clients. Noting that until recently, religious writings have tended to reflect a male-centered bias and patriarchal values, issues related to women's spirituality are identified, implications for therapeutic interventions are discussed, and a model for understanding and facilitating women's spirituality is proposed. *[Article copies available for a fee from The Haworth Document Delivery Service: 1-800-342-9678. E-mail address: getinfo@haworth.com]*

INTRODUCTION

For many years helping professionals have struggled with the issue of addressing clients' ethical and spiritual values. More than 30 years ago Ellis (1962) hypothesized that "religiosity to a large degree essentially is masochism, and both are forms of mental sickness" (pp. 1-7). A different viewpoint was held by London (1964), who merely noted that therapists gave little attention to psychotherapy as a fundamentally moral enterprise:

Joyce Hickson is Chair of the Department of Counseling and Clinical Programs, Columbus College, Columbus, GA 31907. Andrea Phelps is affiliated with the Northwest Alabama Mental Health Center, Winton County Office, Haleyville, AL.

[Haworth co-indexing entry note]: "Women's Spirituality: A Proposed Practice Model." Hickson, Joyce, and Andrea Phelps. Co-published simultaneously in *Journal of Family Social Work* (The Haworth Press, Inc.) Vol. 2, No. 4, 1997, pp. 43-57; and: *The Family, Spirituality and Social Work* (ed: Dorothy S. Becvar) The Haworth Press, Inc., 1998, pp. 43-57. Single or multiple copies of this article are available for a fee from The Haworth Document Delivery Service [1-800-342-9678, 9:00 a.m. - 5:00 p.m. (EST). E-mail address: getinfo@haworth.com].

[P]sychotherapeutic training programs in psychiatry, psychology, social work–even in the ministry–often do not deal seriously with the problem of morals. Psychotherapeutic literature is full of formal principles of procedures and somewhat vague statements of goals, but it generally says little or nothing about the possible moral implications of these procedures and goals–indeed, it often fails even to mention that there are any moral, as opposed to scientific implications to psychotherapy, though the objective of the latter are rationalized by the former. It is as if therapists were themselves unconscious of some of the most profound difficulties in their own work. (p. 6)

Although generally it still is agreed that practitioners should not impose their value system on clients, more recently Beutler, Crago and Arizmendi (1986) assert that "many authors are urging therapists both to attend to their own religious and attitudinal systems and to be aware of the potential value of those of their patients" (p. 274). The assumption is that to ignore spirituality is to ignore a significant influence on human behavior. As Colangelo (1992) notes, "The process of counseling is strongly a moralistic and value enterprise, as well as a scientific enterprise. Ethics and spirituality are inexorably interwoven into the systematic process of helping clients change" (p. vii).

Shafranske and Gorsuch (1984) conducted a study which examined psychologists' perceptions of spirituality and the profession's preparedness to respond to the spiritual dimension as experienced by clients. Their findings suggest that client issues and behavior, associated with a spiritual or religious context, tend to be addressed in one of two ways: regarded as not relevant or viewed as relevant as understood within the personal spiritual framework of the therapist. Another perspective on the issue of including spirituality in the counseling process is captured by Burke and Miranti (1992) who ask: "Why the resistance and conflict as to whether or not it is proper to explore this dimension in the counseling setting? . . . Can more time be wasted in arguing for or against the need to address this dimension?" (p. 2).

Although the 1960s were referred to as the era of value-free counseling, by the 1980s some attention was being given to transpersonal psychology and the movement to incorporate dimensions of spirituality and religious beliefs into the therapeutic process. Bergin (1992) identifies three ways in which a spiritual perspective may contribute to psychological thought and practice. The first is as a conception of human nature, the second, as a moral frame of reference, and the third, as a set of techniques. Accordingly, the essential centerpiece in a spiritual orientation is that there is a spiritual reality and that spiritual experiences make a difference in the lives of clients. Further, a spiritual orientation anchors values in universal terms and reemphasizes the importance of being open, specific, and deliberate about values. Finally, a spiritual perspective contributes a set of techniques ranging from intrapsychic methods, such as the use of prayer, scripture study, rituals, and inspirational counseling, to those of family and social system methods such as group support, communication, mutual participation, communal spiritual experience, and group identification.

Worthington (1989) presents five reasons which he considers compelling for giving attention to the implications of religious faith in understanding both normal development and remediation. These include:

1. A high percentage of the population in the United States identifies itself as religious.
2. Many people who are undergoing emotional crises consider religion as they manage their dilemmas, even if they have not recently been active in formal religion.
3. Many clients are reluctant to bring up their religious considerations as part of secular therapy.
4. In general, therapists are not as religiously oriented as their clients.
5. As a result of being less religiously oriented than their clientele, many helpers might not be as informed about religion as would be maximally helpful for many of their clients (p. 609).

It is interesting to note that attendance by adults at worship services surpasses weekly professional sports attendance. Additionally, an overwhelming 95% of Americans profess belief in God (Ostling, 1995). It is highly likely, with so many people engaging in religious activities, that most clients seen in therapy have some religious values that influence their behavior. Thus, according to Theodore (1992), "to exclude spirituality is to refuse to look at a very significant influence on human behavior" (p. 20). In order to establish therapeutic goals, social workers, counselors and other helping practitioners need to understand the client's view of what constitutes healthy functioning, and how healthy functioning is promoted or achieved (Bishop, 1992). Cunningham (1983), for example, believes that effective outcomes will be temporary and the benefits of therapy restricted if the therapist does not integrate solutions that take into account spiritual or religious values.

Although many studies continue to focus primarily on emotional, social, and occupational wellness, spiritual wellness is an element of emerging interest in health education and in mental health literature (Chandler, Holden & Kolander, 1992). Andrews (1994) states that "there is a growing consensus among psychiatrists, psychologists, social workers, family therapists and chemical dependency counselors that cultivating a more spiritual outlook on life is the key to long-term well-being" (p. 28). Indeed, a sign of the times is the fact that the trustees of the American Psychiatric Association recently approved a major change in the *Diagnostic and Statistical Manual of Mental Disorders* (1994). Rather than being labeled as delusional or suffering from a severe mental disturbance, patients who bring up spiritual issues now are to be viewed as having a normal and expected problem of life, no different from coping with marital disagreements, bereavement, a career crisis, or an educational difficulty (Andrews, 1994).

SPIRITUALITY DEFINED

Spirituality is a term which appears to connote many meanings. For example, participants at the recent First Invitational Summit on Spirituality in Counseling struggled to come up with a definition or description of spirituality ("Summit results," 1995). That is, each definition of spirituality appears to be very personal. It can be the ability to draw power from a transcendent dimension for some, while for others it is the ability to form a personal relationship with a supreme being. Other definitions point to the sense of connectedness with a supreme being, others and ourselves, or focusing on a personalized journey during which certain people and circumstances encourage our spiritual growth. However, while spirituality is one of the few things we can hold onto as being uniquely our own, we can integrate the definitions, as distinctly separate as they are, to depict a rich spectrum of meaning and faith. As Becvar (1994) notes, "Spirituality refers to a way of being in the world that acknowledges the existence of a transcendent dimension. It includes an awareness of the connectedness of all that is, and accepts that all of life has meaning and purpose and is thus sacred" (p. 14).

Chandler et al. (1992) propose that a definition of spirituality include a sense of spirit, soul, noncorporeality, and sacredness. Their definition allows "for the experience of relationship to a higher power, as well as the experience of "no-thingness" considered to be the epitome of enlightenment in some Eastern traditions" (p. 170). They define spirituality independently of religion, stating that spirituality can occur in or out of the context of the institution of organized religion, and that not all aspects of religion are assumed to be spiritual.

Elkins, Hedstrom, Hughes, Leaf and Saunders (1988) believe there is a need for a humanistic understanding of spirituality. In the clinical arena, a humanistic spirituality can provide practitioners with a legitimate nonreligious approach to the therapeutic treatment of clients suffering from spiritual distress. These authors further define spirituality as " . . . a way of being and experiencing that comes about through awareness of a transcendent dimension, and that is characterized by certain identifiable values in regard to self, others, nature, life, and whatever one considers to be the ultimate" (p. 10). Based on their humanistic model, they also developed an inventory that assesses spirituality more comprehensively and does not equate it with narrow religious beliefs, rituals and practices. According to these authors, a definition of spirituality in psychological terminology is that it is a multidimensional construct consisting of nine major components.

The first component is the transcendent dimension, with the actual content ranging from the traditional view of a personal God to a psychological view that the "transcendent" dimension is simply a natural extension of the conscious self into the regions of the unconscious or Greater Self. The spiritual person, in the second component, has known and emerged from a quest for meaning and purpose in life with confidence that life is deeply meaningful and that one's own existence has purpose. The third component is that the spiritual person feels a sense of responsibility to life, a calling to answer, a mission to accomplish, or in some cases, even a destiny to fulfill. The spiritual person, in the fourth component, believes all of life is infused with sacredness, and experiences often, even in "nonreligious" settings, a sense of awe, reverence, and wonder. In the fifth component, the spiritual person knows that ultimate satisfaction is not found in money and possessions but in spiritual things. In the sixth component, the spiritual person experiences a strong sense of social justice, and is committed to altruistic love and action. The spiritual person, in the seventh component, is committed to high ideals and to the actualization of positive potential in all aspects of life. The spiritual person, in the eighth component, is deeply aware of human pain, suffering and death. Finally, the spiritual person is one whose spirituality has born fruit in his or her life.

We would note at this point that within the context of cultural forces, approaches to spirituality generally have sacralized patriarchal images. Indeed, there is no definitive historical collection of texts that make women's spiritual experience visible. Thus, until recently, religious writings have tended to reflect a male-centered bias and patriarchal values. What is missing is an examination of women's spiritual perspectives. Such perusal has the potential to yield a rich harvest of new motifs and make explicit women's spirit. Social workers, counselors and other practitioners, can benefit by moving beyond prevailing paradigms to a larger understanding of what it means to be human.

WOMEN'S SPIRITUALITY

Increasingly, women's spirituality is recognized as containing distinctive qualities. Differences between men and women in language, life experiences, their experience of God, style of prayer and ways of being are now being recognized (Guenther, 1992). Women's spirituality has been shaped by social, religious and family experiences. Indeed, the assignment of women to secondary status has had profound implications for the formation of their spirituality. Limited in their access to public power, women have exercised influence through the structures permitted by patriarchy. For example, characteristics such as silence, docility, cooperation, deference and dependence have been encouraged in the socialization of women (Lewis, Hayes, & Bradley, 1992) while initiative, resourcefulness, ambition, scholarship, competition, and the like have not. Women have been accorded derivative status through father, husband, son, or the patriarchal ecclesiastical superstructure. Inasmuch as they usually have been measured by the standard of male normativity, it is not surprising that they have been found deficient (Marshall-Green & Hinson, 1990).

In addition, women's exclusion from positions of ministry has affected their self-understanding as here, too, they have been forced into a second-class status. The effects of characterizing God in exclusively male terms also cannot be fully assessed. Man as the glory of God and woman as the glory of man has described an eternal cosmic hierarchy that always places man closer to (and thus more like) God than woman (Reuther, 1983).

A major deterrent to the development of women's spirituality is that women sometimes have been victimized by sexual misconduct within the church. "When a clergy person sexually exploits or abuses a parishioner, they steal both from their body and soul," said Nancy Turner (Foster, 1995, p. 12), coordinator of the assault survivors advocacy program at the University of Northern Colorado. To be victimized and exploited by a clergy person is both confusing and demeaning. According to Ormerod (1995), "The minister's actions can destroy the spiritual life of the woman, making her feel totally unworthy of God's love and forgiveness. She can feel as if God himself has abused her" (p. 25).

In conducting research for his book, *Sex in the Forbidden Zone: When Men in Power–Therapists, Doctors, Clergy, Teachers and Others–Betray Women's Trust*, Peter Rutter (1995) writes that he frequently heard the statement, "It happens all the time." Sharon Foster (1995, p. 12) notes that:

> The Christian message talks about love, forgiveness, healing, justice and mercy, and church leaders can articulate that message with all the eloquence of angels. But in the area of sexual abuse by its

ministers, church officials too often prove themselves capable only of talk, not action. They get caught up in patterns of behavior which serve to "protect" perpetrators and further harm survivors. They put the financial and public relations concerns of the church before the demands of justice for those who have suffered at the hands of church leaders.

According to Rutter (1995, p. 75), the sexual exploitation of female parishioners probably will continue:

> Given that there are fewer mechanisms for professional accountability for those in ministry, that they have no clear code of professional ethics and that their training in counseling skills are minimal, it would come as no surprise if ministers were to have a worse record than secular professionals.

Finally, the wounding effect of being sexually victimized by clergy and its impact on women's spiritual development is depicted by Ormerod (1995, p. 122) as follows:

> The minister stands as God's representative to God's people and so when he acts in a sexually abusive manner to a woman there are inevitable consequences for women's spiritual life and personal development. Often women who are so affected drift away from the church and lose any spiritual sense. This is all the more treacherous given that women will often approach a minister precisely because he offers the hope of some spiritual guidance and insight. (p. 122)

Many women do indeed seek therapy and help for their brokenness. However, regardless of whether or not they have endured the agony of sexual abuse by clergy, women often have been caught up in the patriarchal aspect of their church. When faced with a need to discover their own spirituality, women find that their faith and their experience of God are totally inadequate in fulfilling their present needs and in aiding them to become fulfilled women (Ochs, 1983; Randour, 1987). The neat compartmentalized image of the God they have lived with is no longer acceptable. Women therefore may need to find a new way to define God, apart from the "father" or "male" image they grew up with, and often separate from any sexual abuse they may have experienced at the hands of clergy.

Thus, a major problem is that women often attempt to live out inauthentic stories provided by a culture they did not create. As Christ (1980, p. 1) writes:

Women's stories have not been told. And without stories there is no articulation of experience. Without stories a woman is lost when she comes to make the important decisions of her life. She does not learn to value her struggles, to celebrate her strengths, to comprehend her pain. Without stories she cannot understand herself. Without stories she is alienated from those deeper experiences of self and world that have been called spiritual or religious. She is closed in silence. The expression of women's spiritual quest is integrally related to the telling of women's stories. If women's stories are not told, the depth of women's souls will not be known.

Until recently the study of spirituality has been equated with the study of men, and women have been ignored as subjects of research. However, while it is necessary to include them, rather than merely comparing women to men, it also would be appropriate to focus attention on women's lives and how they experience the world. As Randour (1987) notes:

All extant theologies are incomplete because, just like our psychological theories, they are based primarily on the experience of men. We will not have a complete understanding of the divine reality and our relationship to it, and to each other . . . until our theologies have considered and used the experience of women. (p. 16)

A reconstructed framework is slowly emerging as the detrimental effects of patriarchy on everyone, especially on women, are realized. Similarly, the role of men and women and the implications for their respective spiritual development must be examined. Women's spirituality can be supported if both women and men make progress in a twofold process. First of all, women must "re-examine presuppositions about human development, discover the history of women's experience and leadership that has never been told, and explicate the women-liberating insights implicit in biblical teaching about God" (Conn, 1980, p. 299). Secondly, these aspects must then be incorporated into every aspect of life and ministry.

Indeed, human development models generally have not incorporated a full humanity for women. Kohlberg's theory of moral development (1962) has been criticized for its assumption that a morality based on individual rights, with its emphasis on separation and its requirement for formal abstract thinking, is superior to those moral judgments that are based on a sense of responsibility to self and others. Gilligan's (1982) more interpersonal context of moral decision-making emphasizes connection, not separation, and posits that the self cannot be separated from its impact on others' lives. The notion that spirituality exists within the context of an interpersonal matrix is particularly relevant to women's lives.

A major contribution women make to spiritual perspectives relates to their interconnectedness and awareness of community. For example, within the context of the mother-child relationship, women experience themselves as the recipients of "mothering." Later, as the life-bearers themselves, women begin the process of de-centering the self. This process provides a fertile field and starting point for later spiritual development. It also prepares women for the role of caretaker, which has been assigned to them by their culture, and entails ongoing concern and care. Motherhood and caretaking provide a special context for experiencing a variety of roles. However, it is not only in birthgiving that women experience their humanity, but also in their roles of caring for partners and friends as well as for the aged and dying. In the course of caring for both the living and the dying, women become acutely aware of the passages of life and their own mortality. These experiences provide a great opportunity for a renewed spirituality. In "relational" spirituality, women find meaning and construct a self forged by a world of relationships. As Ochs (1983) has described it, "When we speak of an individual (woman) . . . we are actually referring to a conglomerate" (p. 111).

Growing up female in a society that devalues females does not describe a conducive environment for human development. Women's less than advantageous position in society has, nonetheless, resulted in the development of a women's culture with many exemplary characteristics. The pain of suffering has led to a deeper appreciation of life and a greater compassion toward others. Nevertheless, for most women in a male-dominated society, the representation of God and spiritual symbols-concepts must be recreated.

A WOMEN'S SPIRITUALITY MODEL

A woman's spiritual quest involves asking such basic questions as: Who am I? Why am I here? What is my place in the universe? It is important to acknowledge that men may ask similar questions and that in the attempt to understand how women experience the world, women's and men's experiences cannot be dichotomized solely along gender lines. However, there are certain aspects of the human situation that have been experienced more by women and which are less obvious in the experience of men. There is indeed a feminine spiritual perspective. Thus, in response to questions regarding existence, a woman must first listen to her own voice and respond in light of her own experience. Women must describe the reality of their own world.

The forces that impact most on the lives of women are the energies of life and regeneration. Nurturance as a power of life must be celebrated, and menstruation, childbirth and menopause can be viewed as both developmentally and spiritually significant events. For women to understand their spiritual nature they must first understand their own grounding in nature and natural energies. In beginning their spiritual quest, however, most women must first experience a distinctive form of "nothingness," captured in a sense of self-negation and internalized negative societal messages. This moment of nothingness precedes and becomes a process which leads to ever-deepening insights and new affirmations of selfhood. From this perspective, learning to value being a woman and establishing a positive identity are key parts of a woman's spiritual journey. "Feminism" is not simply a social movement, it is also a profoundly spiritual journey. As Shange (1976) describes, "I found God in myself . . . and I loved her fiercely" (p. 146).

Recognizing their connections with other women and being attuned to their "stories" helps women change the paternalistic world view in which they are embedded. As women begin to construct their own reality, new life possibilities emerge from a new understanding of self and a new orientation to the world. This spiritual quest represents a drive toward wholeness and toward healing the wounds of self-negation. As part of their life story women may recognize the connection between spirituality and personal and social change.

Harris (1989) presents women's spirituality as a "Dance of the Spirit," a rhythmic series of movements, which unlike the steps of a ladder or a staircase, do not go up or down. Instead, the steps of women's spiritual lives are much like those in a dance, where there is movement backward and forward, turning and returning, bending and bowing, circling and spiraling. There is no need to finish the dance except in a woman's own good time, and God's. At whatever step a woman finds herself, she is exactly where she is meant to be. Leaning into and living into any one of the steps is the only way to understand the meaning of the dance. Moving on to a next step happens according to the soul's own rhythm, similar to bodily rhythms natural to women.

The first of Harris' seven steps is that of *awakening.* For some women, awakening is precipitated by a crisis such as a divorce or death of a significant other, or a shift in the direction of one's life. Awakening also occurs for many women when they realize a sense of personal identity and an awareness of the presence of self. *Discovering* is the second step and is a way of looking around and seeing or noticing what is there in one's spirituality. In this step, many women lay aside traditional teachings and discover new images of the divinity which take on life and meaning and which are uniquely present in their own lives. According to Harris, discovering, in essence, is a "theology of revelation" and women accordingly take what they find and gently mold the findings into a shape fitting for them as spiritual creatures in their world and reality. The third step is *creating*, which involves a process similar to Langer's (1942) artistic model: (1) contemplating the material of one's life; (2) engaging and interacting with it; (3) reforming it into a new whole; and finally (4) allowing this "stuff" to emerge and release into the world. *Dwelling*, the fourth step, involves a tuning out of the outer world and a tuning in to the inner presence. This abiding characteristic occurs after spirituality has taken shape and become formed or created. A fifth step is *nourishing*, which integrates the previous elements and feeds the spirit. Harris refers to nourishing activities as "calisthenics for the soul," such as prayer, contemplation, meditation, journal writing, fasting, etc. *Traditioning*, a sixth step, is referred to by Harris as "generativity," and a desire to guide and spiritually mentor the next generation. Women have a responsibility to educate and initiate others into their own spirituality. Finally, women are impelled to go beyond themselves and their families to a spirituality that cares for the universe. In the last *transforming* step, a woman's spirituality culminates in becoming a steward of the entire cosmos. To Harris, when this step is reached, women can stop for awhile, but only to realize that they have reached the time to begin the dance once more, at a deeper, more fundamental level, in a never-ending rhythm of awakening, discovering, creating, dwelling, nourishing, traditioning, and transforming.

ADDRESSING WOMEN'S SPIRITUALITY: A PROPOSED PRACTICE MODEL

Women's spiritual development is not confined to religious organizations but also can be facilitated in the context of the therapeutic process. The search for spiritual understanding is a process of discovery in which "relational" dialogue between the practitioner and client can play a significant part. Therapy can help women discover essential truths and answer some of life's most basic questions. It is proposed that salient themes and relevant issues be addressed as follows:

Exploration. Women must feel free to express who they are without first looking for approval from others. Since they have been conditioned to look toward an external male authority, they also are influenced heavily by cultural and religious ideas about the role of women in society, images of God, the nature of sin, and other theological issues. In order to mature spiritually, women must shift from an external framework to their own internal authority. Social workers, counselors and other practitioners can help women to stop looking outside themselves for direction and to turn inside and listen to their own voice.

Interdependence. Women also live in a world of interpersonal relationships. In aiding women in their spiritual journey, it may be important to acknowledge that the concept of self for women is really "self-in-relation." Instead of developing a therapeutic goal which emphasizes independence, recognition might be given to a spiritual dimension that involves the capacity for relationships. Such relationships are a practical dimension of spirituality in the everyday lives of women. Practitioners can employ a model that focuses on relationships as a context for spirituality.

Balance. Women may need a mechanism for handling the demands of others while at the same time pursuing their own opportunities for soul development. They may need "desert experiences" where they retreat from the world and contemplate the nature of God and their place in the universe. Practitioners can aid a female client in discovering and acknowledging previously unknown parts of herself. These must be differentiated and then integrated into a larger self vision. The dialectic of meeting the needs of others and responding to the self's own needs must be achieved.

Transformation. The cleansing of pain and anger regarding their inferior status should be an integral part of the ongoing process of women's spiritual development. "Letting go" is necessary in order for women to see the full potential of their spiritual existence. Such surrender paves the way for a new level of spiritual understanding. This does not mean that women adopt a doormat mentality, but rather that they hold the wound up to the light for healing. Practitioners can enable female clients to explore their own vulnerability. Taking such a risk allows women to experience themselves in special ways. It also frees them to have a different kind of spiritual relationship that is an enriching and freeing experience, and can lead to a deeper spiritual journey.

Wholeness. Issues for those women who have been victimized by clergy persons include: anger, grief, shame, betrayal and confusion. The victim feels both rage and hurt at having been exploited and betrayed. A devastating emotional aftermath can be the result. This can be even more traumatic for those women who also formerly were abused by their father or spouse. Such victims of clergy sexual abuse must sort through personal feelings of self-doubt and vulnerability, as well as the trauma of having been violated by a "spiritual" source whom they trusted, admired and on whom they relied. Because many clerical perpetrators are highly respected in both the church and community, parishioners can have a difficult time comprehending the clergy person's actions. Victims may feel unworthy, guilty, and full of self-doubt. To be sexually violated is extremely damaging. To be violated by someone who occupies a church leadership position is even more horrific and can destroy the spiritual life of a woman. Therapy can intervene positively by helping the sexual victim to explore and understand power, trust and boundary issues while providing a safe and special place where therapist/client non-sexual intimacy encounters can take place. Despite these therapeutic interventions, however, the emotional wounds of the experience of cleric sexual misconduct may forever prohibit a woman from again seeking sanctuary and enlightenment within the church.

CONCLUSION

The issue of addressing spiritual values in therapy has been problematic for many years. Clients undergoing emotional crises, however, often give consideration to the religious and spiritual domain as they attempt to come to terms with their dilemmas. Furthermore, spiritual wellness is an emerging element of interest in the field of social work as well as mental health practice in general. Increasingly, spirituality is receiving attention as is an emphasis on the spirituality of women. The social experience of women has had profound implications for the development of their spirituality. The spiritual quest for women contains distinct qualities and can be facilitated through the therapeutic process. Relevant themes and issues may be those of exploration, interdependence, balance, transformation and wholeness.

Social workers, counselors, and other mental health professionals also must recognize that a woman's experience and expression of spirituality may be influenced by individual and cultural elements. Accordingly, there is a need for practitioners to understand spiritual beliefs from the perspective of diversity, and to enable each woman not only to self-explore and understand what her religious and spiritual beliefs are, but to accept her own belief system as well. The proposed practice model is provided to facilitate awareness that a woman's spiritual journey is a continuous process, that each woman has a story to tell, and that the helping professional's role is to help each woman find her own voice.

REFERENCES

American Psychiatric Association. (1994). *Diagnostic and statistical manual of mental disorders* (4th ed.). Washington, DC: Author.
Andrews, L. M. (1994). Will organized religion take over addiction treatment? *Professional Counselor, 8*, 26-33.
Becvar, D. (1994, August). Can spiritual yearnings and therapeutic goals be melded? *Family Therapy News*, pp. 13-14.

Bergin, A. E. (1992). Three contributions of a spiritual perspective to counseling, psychotherapy, behavior change. In M. T. Burke & J. G. Miranti (Eds.), *Ethical and spiritual values in counseling* (pp. 5-15). Alexandria, VA: Association for Religious and Value Issues in Counseling.

Beutler, L. E., Crago, M., & Arizmendi, T. G. (1986). Research on therapist's variables in psychotherapy. In S. L. Garfield & A. E. Bergin (Eds.), *Handbook of psychotherapy and behavior change* (pp. 257-310). New York: Wiley.

Bishop, D. R. (1992). Religious values as cross-cultural issues in counseling. *Counseling and Values, 36*, 178-191.

Burke, M. T. & Miranti, J. G. (Eds.). (1992). Ethics and spirituality: The prevailing forces influencing the counseling profession. In M. T. Burke & J. G. Miranti (Eds.), *Ethical and spiritual values in counseling* (pp. 1-4). Alexandria, VA: Association for Religious and Value Issues in Counseling.

Chandler, C. K., Holden, J. M., & Kolander, C. A. (1992). Counseling for spiritual wellness: Theory and practice. *Journal of Counseling and Development, 71*, 168-175.

Christ, C. (1980). *Diving deep and surfacing*. Boston, MA: Beacon Press.

Colangelo, N. (1992). Foreword. In M. T. Burke & J. G. Miranti (Eds.), *Ethical and spiritual values in counseling* (pp. vii). Alexandria, VA: Association for Religious and Value Issues in Counseling.

Conn, J. W. (1980). Women's spirituality: Restriction and reconstruction. *Cross Currents*, pp. 293-308.

Cunningham, S. (1983, December). Spirituality seen as neglected aspect of psychotherapy. *APA Monitor*, p. 21.

Elkins, D. N., Hedstrom, L. J., Hughes, L. L., Leaf, J. A. & Saunders, C. (1988). Toward a humanistic-phenomenological spirituality: Definition, description and measurement. *Journal of Humanistic Psychology, 28*, 5-18.

Ellis, A. (1962, October). The case against religion: A psychotherapist's view. *The Independent*, pp. 1-7.

Foster, S. (1995, December). The sexual exploitation of women by men in power. *Counseling Today, 38* (6), 10-13.

Gilligan, C. (1982). *In a different voice: Psychological theory and women's development*. Cambridge, MA: Harvard University Press.

Guenther, M. (1992). *Holy listening: The art of spiritual direction*. Cambridge, MA: Cowley Publications.

Harris, M. (1989). *Dance of the spirit: The seven steps of women's spirituality*. New York: Bantam Books.

Kohlberg, L. (1962). Continuities in childhood and adult moral development. In P. B. Bates & K. W. Schlae (Eds.), *Life span developmental psychology: Personality and socialization*. (pp. 11-36). New York: Academic Press.

Langer, S. K. (1942). *Philosophy in a new key: A study in the symbolism of person, rite, and art*. Cambridge, MA.: Harvard University Press.

Lewis, J. A., Hayes, B. A., & Bradley, L. J. (1992). *Counseling women over the life span*. Denver, CO: Love Publishing Co.

London, P. (1964). *The modes and morals of psychotherapy.* New York: Holt, Rinehart and Winston.

Marshall-Green, M. T., & Hinson, E. G. (1990). The contribution of women to spirituality. In B. J. Leonard (Ed.), *Becoming Christian: Dimension of spiritual formation*, pp. 116-130. Louisville, KY: Westminster/John Knox Press.

Ochs, C. (1983). *Women and spirituality.* Totowa, NJ: Rowman & Allanheld.

Ormerod, N. (1995). *When ministers sin, sexual abuse in the churches.* Cincinnati, OH: Millennium Books.

Ostling, R. N. (1995, January 30). In so many Gods we trust, *Time*, pp. 72-74.

Randour, M. L. (1987). *Women's psyche, women's spirit.* New York: Columbia University Press.

Reuther, R. (1983). *Sexism and God-talk: Toward a feminist theology.* Boston, MA: Beacon Press.

Rutter, P. (1995). *Sex in the forbidden zone: When men in power—therapists, doctors, clergy, teachers and others—betray women's trust.* New York: Fawcett Press.

Shafranske, E. P., & Gorsuch, R. L. (1984). Factors associated with the perception of spirituality in psychotherapy. *The Journal of Transpersonal Psychology, 16,* 231-241.

Shange, N. (1976). *for Colored girls who have considered suicide/when the rainbow is enough.* New York: Macmillan.

Summit results in formation spirituality competencies. (1995, December). *Counseling Today, 38* (6), 30.

Theodore, R. M. (1992). Utilization of spiritual values in counseling: An ignored dimension. In M. T. Burke & J. T. Miranti (Eds.), *Ethical and spiritual values in counseling* (pp. 17-22). Alexandria, VA: Association for Religious and Value Issues in Counseling.

Worthington, E. L. Jr., (1989). Religious faith across the lifespan: Implications for counseling and research. *Counseling Psychologist, 17,* 555-612.

A Qualitative Investigation
of the Meaning
# of Religion and Spirituality
to a Group of Orthodox Christians:
Implications for Marriage
and Family Therapy

Charles Joanides, MDiv, MA

SUMMARY. Religion and spirituality have recently become topics of discussion among marital and family therapists as well as other mental health professionals. This article attempts to contribute to the ongoing discussion by presenting descriptions and interpretations from a qualitative study that involved fifteen self-described Eastern Orthodox Christians. Respondents were asked to offer their perceptions of the terms religion and spirituality. Domain analysis suggests that these respondents perceive a profound connection between the terms religion and spirituality. Results also suggest that social workers and other practitioners who work with self-described religious families may be missing some salient information when they (a) fail

Charles Joanides is Pastor of St. Demetrios Greek Orthodox Church, Waterloo, IA. He is also a doctoral student in the Marriage and Family Therapy Program at Iowa State University, Department of Human Development and Family Studies, Ames, IA 50011-1120.

The author wishes to thank Michael Bell, PhD, and Dorothy S. Becvar, MSW, PhD, for their insightful suggestions, support and encouragement.

[Haworth co-indexing entry note]: "A Qualitative Investigation of the Meaning of Religion and Spirituality to a Group of Orthodox Christians: Implications for Marriage and Family Therapy." Joanides, Charles. Co-published simultaneously in *Journal of Family Social Work* (The Haworth Press, Inc.) Vol. 2, No. 4, 1997, pp. 59-76; and: *The Family, Spirituality and Social Work* (ed: Dorothy S. Becvar) The Haworth Press, Inc., 1998, pp. 59-76. Single or multiple copies of this article are available for a fee from The Haworth Document Delivery Service [1-800-342-9678, 9:00 a.m. - 5:00 p.m. (EST). E-mail address: getinfo@haworth.com].

59

to address religious and spiritual factors, and (b) choose to dichoto-mize religion and spirituality when working with self-described religious clients and their families. *[Article copies available for a fee from The Haworth Document Delivery Service: 1-800-342-9678. E-mail address: getinfo@haworth.com]*

A small but growing number of marital and family therapists (MFTs) have recently begun to discern the affect that religion and spirituality has on individuals and families (Becvar, 1994; Berenson, 1990; Boszormenyi-Nagy, Grunebaum & Ulrich, 1991; Butler, 1988; Coleman, Kaplan & Downing 1986; Dan, 1990; Friedman, 1985; Goldberg, 1994; Griffith, 1986; Krone, 1983; Kudlac, 1991; Prest & Keller, 1994; Ross, 1994; Stander, Piercy, Mackinnon & Helmeke, 1994; Stewart & Gale, 1994; Whipple, 1987). Despite the relative newness of this literature, many convincing arguments have been generated that both encourage and justify the inclusion of religious and spiritual concerns during marital and family therapy. This discussion has generated an ongoing dialogue between MFTs who are interested in incorporating their clients' religious and spiritual experiences into the therapeutic process.

As this conversation has developed, however, a rather inconspicuous, yet significant inconsistency appears to have emerged within the present body of literature. Specifically, some MFTs who include religious and spiritual concerns into the therapeutic context tend to treat these terms as separate entities (Boszormenyi-Nagy et al., 1990; Friedman, Goldberg, 1994; 1985; Kudlac, 1991; Stewart & Gale, 1994). Other MFTs appear to circumvent religious concerns and prefer to focus most of their attention on spiritual concerns (Becvar, 1994; Butler, 1988; Griffith, 1986; Prest & Keller, 1994). Still others choose to focus attention on religious/cultural issues and appear to de-emphasize an examination of the spiritual experience of individuals or families (Stander et al., 1994).

Though the differences may appear irrelevant at first glance, when clinicians choose to employ one of these approaches in the work that they do with religious clients, they may inadvertently be disallowing crucial information to enter the therapeutic context. For example, it may be that self-described religious people do not view or experience religion and spirituality in dichotomous terms. As such, approaches that fail to appre-hend the gestalt that exists between the terms religion and spirituality may provide a skewed and incomplete perspective of this population's lived experience and may be negatively affecting both the quality and length of marital and family therapy with self-described religious people.

In an effort to begin investigating these tentative assumptions and con-cerns, a qualitative study was conducted with fifteen self-described religious people. To be more specific, this study sought to present an empathic understanding (Weber, 1968) of the terms religion and spirituality from religious people's observations and interpretations of the terms religion and spirituality. An equally important purpose of this study was to develop a thick description (Geertz, 1973) of the terms religion and spirituality from this population's perspective. And finally, the study attempted to apprehend the interconnectedness (if any) that religious people perceive between the terms religion and spirituality. It was hoped that such an investigation might serve to amplify a voice that has otherwise been peripheral or none-existent within the current body of MFT literature in which ways to incorporate religious and spiritual concerns into the therapeutic context are being explored. It was also anticipated that this investigation might enhance the theoretical grounding that currently informs the work that MFTs and other practitioners do with religious clients and families, thereby improving their effectiveness.

Initially, a brief discussion of the value and purpose of qualitative research as applied to marriage and family therapy will be presented. An overview of the methodology employed in this study will then be detailed, followed by an explanation of the procedures used to analyze the data. A listing and detailed examination of the results will subsequently be offered. Finally, a discussion of the results as applied to MFTs and others who work with religious clients will be provided along with conclusions and recommendations for further research.

QUALITATIVE RESEARCH

Anthropologists and sociologists have successfully used a qualitative research approach for several decades (Vidich & Lyman, 1994). Recently, educators and other social scientists have also discerned the value of using this research paradigm (Denzin & Lincoln, 1994). Among this latter group are a growing number of MFTs who have begun to discover the value and utility of this form of inquiry (Joanning, Newfield & Quinn, 1987; Moon, Dillon & Sprenkle, 1990; Newfield, Kuehl, Joanning & Quinn, 1990; Piercy, Moon & Bischof, 1994; Sells, Smith, Coe, Yoshioka & Robbins, 1994; Sells, Smith & Sprenkle, 1995; Smith, Sells, & Clevenger, 1994). Some of the salient reasons often cited to support the adoption and use of a qualitative approach are as follows. First, qualitative research is emergent and discovery-oriented and has proven to be useful in generating theory and enhancing quantitative research (Joanning et al., 1987; Moon et al., 1990; Sells et al., 1995). Second, qualitative research tends to be heuristic in character and serves to provide new, broad perspectives of complex human systems (Newfield et al., 1990; Sells et al., 1994, 1995). Third, qualitative research provides a thick, rich description of a given human system's lived experience (Newfield et al., 1990). Fourth, in light of the increasingly prominent place that interpretative, postmodern, feminist, and multicultural thinking holds within the MFT field, the value and worth of this form of inquiry has proven indispensable (Moon et al., 1990). To be more specific, since the assumption is made that there is no one clear lens through which the world can be viewed, and everyone's perceptions of the world are filtered through such lenses as those of gender, language, race, class, ethnicity and religion, MFTs have found a qualitative approach useful when attempting to describe the stories imbedded in human systems or to capture their points of view. Fifth, since this method of inquiry is emergent and discovery-oriented, it has been found to be user-friendly when researchers are attempting to study complex systems (Joanning et al., 1987; Moon et al., 1990; Newfield et al., 1990; Piercy et al., 1994; Sells et al., 1994a; Sells et al., 1995; Smith et al., 1994).

METHODOLOGY

Description of the Researcher's Role

I have been a Greek Orthodox priest for fifteen years and have had occasion to serve several Greek Orthodox churches. During my ministerial tenure I have enjoyed network connections and rapport with numerous Orthodox Christians. I thus decided to obtain participants for the study from this population. I could think of no specific reasons why this sampling procedure would provide skewed descriptions and interpretations that would ultimately affect this study's transferability to other similar groups. It should also be noted that this type of purposive and convenience sampling has proven to be sufficient when researchers seek to document beliefs and behavior patterns that occur within social settings (Newfield et al. 1990; Strauss & Corbin, 1994).

From the outset of this study I was cognizant of how my role as an Orthodox priest, whether friend or colleague, might affect the quality of the information gathered. To help reduce respondent bias, a therapeutic technique was employed that is sometimes used by clinicians to minimize the effects of certain latent, inhibiting influences during the therapeutic process. Specifically, during the interview process I chose "to make the covert, overt" (Watzlawick, Weakland & Fisch, 1974) and I indicated that my role as priest, friend or colleague might bias my respondents' answers.

Description of Sampling Technique and Respondents

I purposively selected fifteen Eastern Orthodox respondents to participate in this study. The sample was limited to 15 because the investigator
determined that a saturation point in the data collection had been achieved
toward the end of the interviewing process as no substantially new information was being gathered. Eight respondents were females and seven
were males. Female respondents' ages ranged between 27-78, with a mean
age of 41; male respondents' ages ranged between 34-65, with a mean age
of 44. All were Caucasian, and nearly 70% identified themselves as
Greek-Americans who had been born into the Orthodox faith. The remain-
ing 30% were either converts who had married into the Orthodox faith or
who had left another faith tradition to become a part of the Orthodox
Church. Most respondents were professionals who possessed advanced
degrees in the fields of computer science, economics, education, ethics,
medicine, music, theology or law. Several were business people, and two
identified themselves as homemakers. Each respondent was also a self-described Orthodox Christian. Respondents were selected on the basis of
their leadership role, active participation in their respective churches, and
the researcher's perception of each individual's ability to expound upon
the terms religion and spirituality from an Orthodox Christian perspective.
Respondents who eventually agreed to participate in this study lived in
Connecticut, Iowa, Louisiana, Massachusetts, New York and Oklahoma.

Description of Interview Techniques

In an effort to generate descriptions and interpretations for this study, I
decided to conduct both face-to-face interviews and telephone interviews.
The reasons for the adoption and implementation of these two interviewing techniques were that (a) the questions (see Appendix A) asked were
philosophical in nature and were judged to be appropriately suited to both
telephone and face-to-face interviewing techniques; (b) the research design called for selecting knowledgeable respondents whose interpretations
would provide this study with a thick, rich description; and (c) this was a
practical and efficient method to obtain knowledgeable respondents.

A conscious tracking process was also adopted to ensure that the quality of information generated was not being compromised by either of these
two interviewing techniques. For approximately every three interviews
that were conducted by telephone, one face-to-face interview was conducted as a means of juxtaposing the data gathered in both ways. The
information generated by telephone proved to be of equal or better quality
than the information from the four face-to-face interviews. Additionally,

although telephone interviews exclude valuable information such as body language and facial expressions, the use of an auditory medium seemed to enrich the process of data collection by offering a different context from which to investigate this topic of concern. It may have been less inhibiting and more conducive to providing respondents room for introspection. It should also be pointed out here that MFTs and other clinicians have endorsed the value and use of the telephone during intake sessions (Hines, 1994; Selvini, Boscolo, Cecchin & Prata, 1978; Springer, 1991), attesting to the effectiveness of an auditory medium in their efforts to gather information and to include key members in the therapeutic process when distance prohibits them from being in the therapy room.

Types of Questions

A semi-structured questionnaire was utilized (see Appendix B) for the interviews. Before beginning, each respondent was given a brief explanation regarding the purpose of this research. Close-ended questions were subsequently utilized to obtain some demographic information about each respondent; open-ended questions were used to elicit as much information as possible from the respondents' perspectives without intentionally influencing their observations. For example, the researcher asked, "What is your definition of religion from your religious tradition?" If the respondent was able to answer this question, the researcher listened attentively and empathically while being careful not to lead the respondent. If the respondent was unable to answer the question, the interviewer proceeded to the next question. After the interviewer completed each interview, member checking and debriefing (see Appendix B) were conducted.

Other Techniques Used

Qualitative researchers employ a variety of research techniques and data sources to achieve triangulation (Lincoln & Guba, 1985). This is done to cross check data and interpretations to ensure that the conclusions of a given study adequately represent respondents' constructions. To this end, the following additional decisions were made in the researcher's efforts to develop a thick, rich description of respondents' perceptions of the terms religion and spirituality.

I chose to audio tape and transcribe all face-to-face interviews. This decision was made to allow me an opportunity to retain good eye contact with respondents during these interviews. Conversely, since good eye contact was not a concern during the telephone interviews, field notes and member checks were exclusively utilized. In short, because telephone conversations emphasize audio information, I felt freer to focus more of my attention on listening and keeping good field notes rather than on keeping good eye contact.

Together with the audio tapes, transcriptions and field notes that were generated during these interviews, member checks and debriefing were conducted after each interview. Member checking requires that the researcher go back to the respondent when he/she has any questions regarding the information received during the initial interview. Member checks are also used to ensure that the researcher has accurately captured the essence of each respondent's descriptions and interpretations. Debriefing is utilized in an effort to improve the interview process by feeding back information from the respondent's perspective to the interviewer/researcher regarding the interview process. Through this technique the interviewer's style, as well as the content of the questions being asked, can be co-structured and improved as the research process evolves. Both of these techniques have been successfully used in other qualitative research to bolster its trustworthiness (Brigham, 1995; Kuehl, Newfield & Joanning, 1990; Lashley, 1993). A diary was also kept to help the researcher review and summarize each respondent's answers, generate some initial impressions from each respondent's interpretations, critique his own effort as an interviewer, establish an audit trail, and facilitate a peer debriefing process.

Since this investigation was conducted concurrent with a qualitative research methods class that the researcher was taking, members of this class were utilized as peer debriefers, and the professor was utilized as an external auditor. Peer debriefers reviewed the research design and field notes and contributed to the investigator's growing insights through their suggestions and questions. The external auditor reviewed the research protocol, field notes, and conclusions and confirmed that the interpretations were consistent with the data collected.

Analysis

A modified domain analysis as defined by Spradley (1979), and a grounded theory approach as defined by Strauss and Corbin (1994), were utilized during the collection and analysis of data. Specifically, after several readings of the transcripts, field notes and researcher's diary, the researcher began collapsing data into related categories of meaning, i.e., into categories that consisted of related descriptions and interpretations. Second, these categories of meaning were then collapsed into broader emergent domains of meaning and classified with cover terms. Third, these domains of meaning were eventually collapsed under broader, more emergent domains and reclassified with new cover terms. Insights from member checks, peer debriefers and the external auditor helped the researcher during the classification and reclassification process. In total, data analysis generated three domains that will be discussed separately below.

RESULTS

Domain 1: Religion Is More Than a Set of External Rules and Regulations

Respondents' animated and troublesome attempts at defining the term religion were suggestive of the multifaceted character of this term. Because of the complex nature of this term most respondents expressed some initial frustration in their efforts to arrive at a comprehensive definition, and simply offered a series of disjointed descriptions and interpretations. Despite the disjointed nature of many respondents' remarks, however, similar statements surfaced repeatedly throughout the interviews, attesting to certain common perceptions that Eastern Orthodox Christians hold about religion. What follows are the main ideas expressed by the respondents in this study when they were asked to define the term religion.

Respondents consistently felt that a definition of the term religion should embody more than "a set of esoteric rules and regulations" and more than "beliefs and practices." While admittedly rules, rituals and dogma served to describe a dimension of their Orthodox religious experience, the metaphors they consistently employed alluded to a broader, deeper dimension of the term religion. For example, one respondent succinctly stated, "religion is a way of life . . . a path that leads to God's light." Another indicated that religion is like "an eye from which everything is interpreted." In short, these and other similar metaphors appeared to suggest that the term religion was perceived as a broad and encompassing concept that provided these respondents with an Orthodox Christian paradigm from which to make sense of the world.

A pronounced emphasis was also repeatedly placed on the importance of the Orthodox Church's concept of "Holy Tradition," i.e., the religious traditions and teaching that have been passed down "from generation to generation through the Holy Spirit." For example, one metaphor likened religion to a journey where one "walks with centuries of experience." Another respondent spoke at length of the importance of tradition, and how "the Orthodox Church's 2000 year history provides [her] with a sense of continuity and stability." In another interview a respondent stated,

> knowing that things have not changed comforts me . . . knowing that people have celebrated the same liturgy, sacraments, theology for

2000 years provides me with an anchor . . . I don't like the fact that churches are changing things to please their congregations and hold onto their faithful.

And finally, one respondent stated, "[Holy Tradition] provides a mystical continuity with the past. It provides one with a membership in a social organism that transcends the present moment and facilitates a relationship between the saints who have passed on and the Holy Trinity." In these and other instances respondents' remarks, together with subsequent member checks, suggested that a dimension of their religious experience (labeled as Holy Tradition) mystically connected them with their ancestral, cultural and religious roots.

Respondents also tended to repeatedly use the terms "framework" and "structure" in their efforts to describe how they defined this term. Several respondents stated that religion was like "a framework" that helped them "find God" or "communicate with a Higher Energy." These remarks appeared to be suggestive of one of the benefits that is commonly associated with religion: that religion affords religious people with a religious catechetical framework from which to worship God.

Several other respondents also maintained that a definition of religion must contain a moral component, since religion functions to "teach you everything good about life." In these instances, when respondents discussed the moral dimension of their Orthodox religion, they also associated it with the efforts of a "loving and merciful God . . . who seeks to provide us with a moral framework."

Additionally, respondents indicated that religion appeared to assist them in their interpersonal relationships with "their family, friends and neighbors . . . and with God" and thus felt that a definition of religion should also contain this emphasis. Speaking on this subject one respondent stated, "it [his religious experience] is not just a personal relationship with God . . . but a collective and personal relationship." Another respondent stated, "when I'm in Church I feel a part of something–something incomprehensible and mystical–that is greater than me that includes neighbor and God."

To summarize, though respondents in this study failed to construct a comprehensive definition of the term religion, any definition of the term religion from the perspective of these participants would contain some mention of (a) religion's ability to connect them with their past and present, (b) religion's stress upon moral guidelines, (c) religion's ability to superimpose structure and framework upon their spiritual experience, (d) religion's catechetical, moral character, (e) religion's role in their spiritual development, and (f) religion's central role in helping them to make sense of the world.

Although most respondents resonated well with the term religion when they were asked for their perceptions and interpretations of this term, it should also be noted that three respondents initially hesitated and appeared to react with some general discomfort. Member checking after each interview helped me develop a clearer perception of the source of this discomfort. Specifically, these respondents stated that the term "faith . . . or Orthodox Faith" was a more appropriate choice when discussing their perceptions of "Orthodoxy." For example, one respondent stated, "it [religion] is a bad choice of terms . . . it is a dry and lifeless term in my mind . . . I like to use the term faith." In this case the respondent seemed to suggest that this term was more appropriately suited to "formal, academically oriented" discussions. He further described several previous "unfulfilling philosophical debates . . . early in life" that had left him "depleted and cynical." Another respondent reacted similarly stating, "[the term religion] reminds me of my cultural past . . . I link [the term religion] to the spiritually dead church holidays I celebrated with my family [of origin] in Greece as a child . . . I like using the term faith or Orthodox Faith." And still another respondent pointed out that many people can be religious and never manage to allow the essence of their religious experience to "touch the heart or deepest center of their emotions." In this case this respondent was pointing to the "perfunctory, . . . legalistic, . . . magical, . . . religiously immature" attitudes that many religious and non-religious people have adopted about religion. As a result, in an effort to distinguish between religious and nominally religious people, this respondent also preferred to use the term faith. All of which suggests that some religious people may prefer using the term faith rather than the term religion when they identify and discuss their religious persuasions.

It should be pointed out that none of these respondents was anti-religious. On the contrary, as indicated above, all were self-described Orthodox Christians who took active and visible roles in their respective churches. Member checks verified that these reactions to the term religion were an attempt by these respondents to describe certain temporary distractions that had prevented them from developing a deeper religious and spiritual commitment at some point in their religious and spiritual development as well as an attempt to describe some of the challenges that they continue to grapple with as a result of being actively religious. As another respondent pointed out, "being religious in a materialistic society poses a major problem . . . the temptation is always there to seek after the letter of the law, and not the spirit and truth of things . . . Orthodox Christians being no exception." These and other similar reactions are suggestive of the multi-leveled complexity of the term religion, as well as the interconnectedness that exists between religious practice and spiritual development, a point that will become clearer below.

Domain 2: Religion and Spirituality
Are Not Separate Experiences

Many respondents had difficulty defining the term spirituality when they considered it apart from their Orthodox religious tradition. For example, a middle aged homemaker stated, "it's [spirituality] an inner feeling . . . but it's more than that." Another middle aged female computer analyst stated, "[spirituality is] being in touch . . . being aware . . . being in communication with Christ/God on an ongoing basis . . . more or less." And finally after stringing together a lengthy litany of metaphors, a priest stated in exasperation, "it's difficult to define–it must be experienced."

When respondents linked this term with their religious experiences, however, they conversed more freely and their descriptions were generally more discernible. For example, a middle aged secretary stated, "Spirituality is what blossoms from within [my Orthodox religious] framework. It's not separate. . . . it works together. . . . I think you have to have [a religious] framework before you can build a spiritual life." In another instance, a middle aged male business person expanded upon these thoughts and stated, "it [spirituality] comes from one's faith . . . it is a personal relationship that is developed with God through one's [Orthodox] faith." A priest and pastor stated, "spirituality is a gift that comes through the acquisition of the Holy Spirit–both of which are received from practicing one's [Orthodox] faith." Similarly, another priest and pastor stated,

> [spirituality] is the way in which we bring our life into a coherent whole with God . . . it gives us meaning . . . it is a relationship with the Divine through a participation in our Orthodox faith . . . orthopraxia [practicing Orthodoxy] leads to a correct orthodoxia [to correct worship].

Finally, a third priest stated, "spirituality is theosis . . . becoming like God through one's Orthodox Faith."

In summary, despite the fact that these interviews failed to produce a comprehensive picture of what might be called Orthodox Spirituality, what became clear is that, (a) the term spirituality seemed far more nebulous and unintelligible to the respondents in this study when considered apart from their religious background, (b) respondents' perceptions of the term spirituality were profoundly connected to their participation in their Orthodox religious tradition, and (c) respondents' personal relationships with God continue to be nurtured through their respective religious involvement.

Domain 3: Religious People Experience Religion
and Spirituality Holistically

Most respondents who attempted to define similarities between the terms religion and spirituality did so by either indicating that the question was not applicable to their experience, or by stating that they perceived no substantial difference between them. For example, one theologian and priest stated that "[separating these two terms] is the American way of thinking . . . [from an Orthodox perspective] religion and spirituality are not fragmented or bifurcated." Moreover, when asked to suggest a better method, this respondent succinctly stated, "perhaps you should investigate how Orthodox define the term faith." A 27 year old female musician stated that, "there is really not much difference in my mind . . . they mirror each other." Additionally, a 57 year old female executive stated, "religion and spirituality are the same in my mind."

Where respondents did offer observations to this question, their remarks appeared to essentially reflect the difficulty that Orthodox Christians may have when attempting to juxtapose these terms. For example, one respondent stated, "I don't see them as similar, but I'm not sure. . . . I have not finished thinking through the connection and similarity between the two." In another instance a respondent stated, "religion leads to spirituality, and spirituality makes one more religious." When asked if he could elaborate upon this statement he declined, stating he could not provide any further information.

Most respondents avoided drawing distinctions between these two terms. Those who saw a distinction offered fragmented descriptions, while almost always disqualifying their observations with remarks such as "but I'm not sure" and "maybe, but I have to think about it." For example, one respondent stated, "religion is a structured/collective experience . . . spirituality is a personal experience . . . but I'm really not sure." Another respondent stated, "religion is a body of practices which don't necessarily relate to the deepest longings within a person; spirituality implies an inner being and is something in tune with the Divine . . . but I haven't thought this out carefully." In a subsequent interview another respondent stated, "religion is a title of what you believe in . . . spirituality brings you much closer [to God] . . . it is not the result of human nature . . . but I really can't say."

These and other comparable descriptions appeared to further support the notion that an incongruity might have existed between the questions that were asked of these respondents and an Orthodox Christian's religious and spiritual lived experiences. To be more specific, even though some respondents ventured to juxtapose these two terms and describe certain subtle differences, they also appeared to be uncomfortable doing so, and would generally disqualify their observations and plead ignorance. As such, it is suspected that a discussion of the differences between these two terms, though consistent with other religious traditions, may never be completely compatible with an Orthodox Christian phenomenological perspective. Moreover, to discuss religion while excluding spirituality and vice versa may function to provide an incomplete perspective of this population's spiritual or religious lived experiences.

In summary, the observations given when respondents attempted to draw some similarities and dissimilarities between these two terms appeared to suggest that Orthodox Christians who are actively involved in their faith tradition do not think in dichotomous terms when discussing or experiencing religion and spirituality. From these respondent's observations, both religion and spirituality appear to be profoundly intertwined with one another given the extent. Moreover, attempts at juxtaposing these terms, though academically interesting, may not only seem artificial and inconsistent with Orthodox Christians' lived religious and spiritual experience, but also may be inconsistent with the way they think about religion and spirituality.

DISCUSSION AND CONCLUSIONS

According to a recent survey of 113,000 people conducted at City University of New York, an estimated 175 million adults describe themselves as religious (Kosmin & Lachman, 1995). Given this and other similar statistics, a growing number of MFTs and other mental health professionals have become interested in how religion and spirituality impact individuals and families. This study has sought to contribute to the conversation regarding religion and spirituality by providing a thick, rich description of these terms from 15 self-described religious respondents. In effect, the researcher hoped that respondents' observations and interpretations would serve to produce a clearer picture of the perceived roles that religion and spirituality play in religious people's lived experience and of the relationship that exists between religion and spirituality as perceived by religious people. To this end, the following salient observations appear to have surfaced from this study.

First, respondent's descriptions concerning religion and spirituality appear to suggest that religion was perceived as more than a set of external rules and regulations, i.e., religion was described as an experience that embodied a mystical component as well as theological and canonical boundaries. Moreover, though rules and regulations certainly were important components of each respondent's religious experience, religion was also likened to "a bonding agent" that connected them to God, their neighbor (neighbor referring to people in their social network) and to their cultural and ancestral past.

Second, respondents' observations and interpretations in this study also clearly indicated that religion occupied a fundamentally central role in their efforts to make sense of the world around them. An analysis of the data suggests that respondents' Orthodox Christian epistemology was inextricably tied to the manner in which they interpreted the world. All of which presumes that religious people's world view is profoundly shaped by their religious and spiritual experiences.

Third, this group of respondents also indicated that the terms religion and spirituality were more similar than dissimilar and they were generally uncomfortable when asked to discuss these terms separately and insisted that the terms were profoundly interrelated. Their descriptions suggested that they are best understood conjointly and attempts at separating them appeared insufficient and inappropriate. Additionally, several respondents suggested that an examination of the term "faith" (or more accurately, "Orthodox Faith") might provide a more useful focus for study.

Fourth, the data appear to indicate that when attempting to incorporate religion and spirituality into the therapeutic process, MFTs and other clinicians who work with self-described religious clients and families should consider a holistic approach rather than a reductionistic approach that tends to either dichotomize these terms or exclude one or the other. A holistic approach to religion and spirituality would recognize that religious people may perceive a definite connection between these two experiences, and that religious people's spirituality may tend to flow directly from their religious commitment. Such an approach would also tend to emphasize the systemic and recursive nature between these two related experiences as well as the impact that both experiences have on a given religious client's life. Such an approach also would allow the client to broach religious and spiritual issues she or he felt were important to the therapeutic process. Furthermore, by adopting a more holistic approach, therapists might be perceived as more respectful and might obtain a broader, more systemic and recursive perspective. The therapeutic conversation also might be enriched with more information and a more accurate picture of the client's lived experience might emerge.

Fifth, data from this study also suggest that those who adopt an integrative or holistic view of religion and spirituality might be less apt to misdiagnose and pathologize certain behaviors and behavioral patterns. By including religious and spiritual concerns in therapy with religious clients, clinical decisions and judgments would be better informed through a broader understanding of this population.

Sixth, recently MFTs have become keenly aware of the subtle, yet important role that gender, ethnicity, race, and other ecological and idiosyncratic individual and family variables exert on human development and family relations. An increased sensitivity to these and other factors has arguably functioned to make marriage and family therapy a more pertinent and respectful process. Similarly, this study suggests that practitioners who work with self-described religious clients and families should seek to discern the role that both religion and spirituality play in these clients' lives.

Finally, further research is needed to determine if the observations offered in this study hold true for other religious denominations or faith traditions. Juxtaposing religious people with nominally religious people in a similar qualitative study may also prove invaluable to efforts to understand the role that religion and spirituality play in religious people's lives. In a similar manner, investigating a clinical sample of religious people's perceptions may also provide useful insights for therapists who choose to include religious and spiritual concerns in the therapeutic process. Furthermore, a qualitative study exploring the term faith might prove worthwhile, since such an approach may provide a more effective means of capturing the gestalt that exists between the terms religion and spirituality as perceived by religious people. Lastly, increasing our understanding of the roles that religion and spirituality play for self-described religious people's lived experience should not only assist in efforts to provide a stronger theoretical undergirding to clinical work with religious people but also may lead to more effective delivery of services.

REFERENCES

Becvar, D. S. (1994). Can spiritual yearnings and therapeutic goals be melded? *Family Therapy News*, June, pp. 13-14.

Berenson, D. (1990). A systemic view of spirituality: God and twelve step programs as resources in Family Therapy, *Journal of Strategic and Systemic Therapies*, *9*, 59-70.

Boszormenyi-Nagy, I., Grunebaum, J., & Ulrich, D. (1991). Contextual Therapy. In A. S. Gurman & D. P. Kniskern (Eds.), *Handbook of Family Therapy: Volume II* (pp. 200-238). New York: Brunner/Mazel.

Brigham, L. (1995). *Therapist conducted debriefing interviews*. Unpublished dissertation, Iowa State University, Ames, Iowa.

Butler, K. (1988). Spirituality reconsidered. *Family Therapy Networker*, *14*, 26-37.

Coleman, S. B., Kaplan, J. D., & Downing, R. W. (1986). Life cycle and loss: The spiritual vacuum of heroin addition. *Family Process*, *25*, 5-23.

Denzin, N. K., & Lincoln, Y. S. (1994). Introduction: Entering the Field of Qualitative Research. In N. K. Denzin & Y. S. Lincoln (Eds.), *Handbook of Qualitative Research* (pp. 1-17). Thousand Oaks, CA: Sage.

Friedman, E. (1985). *Generation to Generation: Family Process in Church and Synagogue.* New York: Guilford Press.

Geertz, C. (1973). *The Interpretation of Cultures.* New York: Basic Books.

Goldberg, J. R. (1994). Spirituality, religion and secular values: What role in psychotherapy? *Family Therapy News,* June, pp. 9, 16-17.

Griffith, J. L. (1986). Employing the God-family relationship with religious families, *Family Process, 25,* 609-618.

Joanning, H., Newfield, N., & Quinn, W. H. (1987). Multiple perspectives for research using family therapy to treat adolescent drug abuse. *Journal of Strategic and Systemic Therapies, 6,* 18-24.

Hines, M. H. (1994). Using the telephone in family therapy. *Journal of Marital and Family Therapy, 20,* 175-184.

Kosmin, B. A., & Lachman, S. P. (1995). Religious self-identification. In K. B. Bedell (Ed.).*Yearbook of American and Canadian Churches 1995.* New York: Abingdon Press.

Krone, L. C. (1983). Justice as a relational and theological cornerstone. *Journal of Psychology and Christianity, 2,* 36-46.

Kudlac, K. E. (1991). Including God in the conversation: The influences of religious beliefs on the problem-organized system. *Family Therapy, 18,* 277-285.

Kuehl, B. P., Newfield, N. A., & Joanning, H. (1990). A client-based description of family therapy. *Journal of Family Psychology, 3,* 310-321.

Lashley, J. (1993). *Informed therapy: Using ethnographic interviews in family therapy.* Unpublished dissertation, Iowa State University, Ames, Iowa.

Lincoln, Y., & Guba, E. (1985). *Naturalistic Inquiry,* Beverly Hills, CA: Sage.

Moon, S. M., Dillon, D. R., & Sprenkle, D. H. (1990). Family therapy and qualitative research, *Journal of Marital and Family Therapy, 16,* 357-373.

Newfield, N. A., Kuehl, B. P., Joanning, H., & Quinn, W. H. (1990). A mini-ethnography of the family of adolescent drug abuse: The ambitious experience. *Alcoholism Treatment Quarterly, 7,* 57-79.

Piercy, F. P., Moon, S. M., & Bischof, G. P. (1994). Difficult journal article reflections among prolific family therapists: A qualitative incident study. *Journal of Marital and Family Therapy, 20,* 231-245.

Prest, L. A., Keller, J. F. (1993). Spirituality and family therapy: Spiritual beliefs, myths and metaphors. *Journal of Marital and Family Therapy, 19,* 137-148.

Sells, S. P., Smith, T. E., Coe, M. J., Yoshioka, M., & Robbins, J. (1994). An ethnography of couple and therapist experiences in reflecting team practice. *Journal of Marital and Family Therapy, 20,* 247-266.

Sells, S. P., Smith, T. E., & Sprenkle, D. H. (1995). Integrating qualitative and quantitative research methods: A research model. *Family Process, 34,* 199-218.

Selvini, M., Boscolo, L., Cecchin, G., & Prata, G. (1978). *Paradox and Counter-*

paradox: A New Model in the Therapy of the Family Schizophrenic Transaction. New York: Jason Aronson.

Smith, T. E., Sells, S. P., & Clevenger, T. (1994). Ethnographic context analysis of couple and therapist perceptions in a reflecting team setting. *Journal of Marital and Family Therapy, 20,* 267-286.

Spradley, J. (1979). *The Ethnographic Interview.* New York, Holt, Rinehart & Winston.

Springer, A. K., (1991). Telephone family therapy: An untapped resource. *Family Therapy, 18,* 123-128.

Stander, V., Piercy, F. P., Mackinnon, D., & Helmeke, K. (1994). Spirituality, religion and family therapy: Competing or complementary worlds? *The American Journal of Family Therapy, 22,* 27-41.

Stewart, S. P. & Gale, J. E. (1994). On hallowed ground: Marital therapy with couples on the religious right. *Journal of Systemic Therapies, 13,* 16-25.

Strauss, A., & Corbin, J. (1994). Grounded theory methodology: An overview. In N. K. Denzin & Y. S. Lincoln, (Eds.), *Handbook of Qualitative Research* (pp. 273-285). Thousand Oaks, CA: Sage.

Vidich, A. J., & Lyman, S. M., (1994). Qualitative research: Their history in Sociology and Anthropology. In N. K. Denzin & Y. S. Lincoln, (Eds.), *Handbook of Qualitative Research* (pp. 23-59). Thousand Oaks, CA: Sage.

Watzlawick, P. Weakland, J. H., & Fisch, R. (1974). *Change.* New York: W. W. Norton.

Weber, M. (1968). The definition of sociology and of social action: A. methodological foundations. In G. Ross & C. Wittich (Eds.), *Economy and Society* (pp. 4-22). CA: University of California Press.

Whipple, V. (1987). Counseling battered women from fundamentalist churches. *Journal of Marital and Family Therapy, 13,* 251-258.

APPENDIX A

Introduction:

I am interested in looking at religion and spirituality. I was hoping that you would agree to answer some questions regarding these two terms from your Orthodox religious tradition. Please also remember that there are no correct answers, and that all answers are correct answers. I also recognize that my role as a Greek Orthodox priest/colleague might influence your answers. If you choose to participate in this study I hope your answers reflect your opinions and are not affected by my role as priest and acquaintance.

Occupation:

Marital Status:

Children:

City, State:

1. What role did religion play as you were growing up?
   (a) What other factors contributed to your formation or development?
2. What role does religion play presently in your life?
3. What is your definition of religion?
4. Given what you have said, how do you understand the term "spirituality" from your religious tradition?
5. What is the difference between the terms religion and spirituality?
6. How do you see these terms as being similar?
7. Any last thoughts or comments?

APPENDIX B

1. What would you change about the interview process?
2. What did you like about the interview process?
3. What would you change about the researcher's interviewing style?
4. What did you like about the researcher's interviewing style?

Spirituality as a Form
of Functional Diversity:
Activating Unconventional
Family Strengths

Karen L. Westbrooks, PhD

SUMMARY. Increasing attention is being given to the role of spirituality in understanding family process. Concerns often focus on the type of clientele for whom spirituality may be of importance, the role of spiritual beliefs in helping to sustain family problems and the sometimes conflicting dynamics between religious identification and spiritual awareness. Assumptions about "what needs to change" dominate literature regarding interventions within spiritual belief systems. This article suggests that consideration for what needs to stay the same also has significant implications for effective practice. If "what needs to stay the same" is inherent in unconventional family strengths we are called to see what may not otherwise be apparent when using traditional ways of knowing. Spirituality emerges from a well-spring of deep culture that is reflected in roles, rules and patterns integral to family life and family survival. *[Article copies available for a fee from The Haworth Document Delivery Service: 1-800-342-9678. E-mail address: getinfo@haworth.com]*

INTRODUCTION

Spirituality as a form of functional diversity is a perspective that emerges from a study of fifty families who listed faith or faith in God as a

Karen L. Westbrooks is Assistant Professor, Western Kentucky University, Bowling Green, KY 42101.

[Haworth co-indexing entry note]: "Spirituality as a Form of Functional Diversity: Activating Unconventional Family Strengths." Westbrooks, Karen L. Co-published simultaneously in *Journal of Family Social Work* (The Haworth Press, Inc.) Vol. 2, No. 4, 1997, pp. 77-87; and: *The Family, Spirituality and Social Work* (ed: Dorothy S. Becvar) The Haworth Press, Inc., 1998, pp. 77-87. Single or multiple copies of this article are available for a fee from The Haworth Document Delivery Service [1-800-342-9678, 9:00 a.m. - 5:00 p.m. (EST). E-mail address: getinfo@haworth.com].

family strength (Westbrooks, 1995). Although findings were based on interviews with low-income families, the implication of the data raises questions regarding the functional role of spirituality in family processes in general. Discussion of spirituality is often relegated to a box called beliefs. The purpose of this article is to challenge the boundaries of that box by suggesting that spirituality is also inherent in roles, rules and patterns that are at the heart of family life and family survival. Five pivotal points of discussion include (1) moving beyond the box into deep culture; (2) spirituality as a form of functional diversity; (3) faith as an unconventional strength; (4) activating unconventional strength; and (5) building on spiritual sameness to effect change.

MOVING BEYOND THE BOX INTO DEEP CULTURE

Prest and Keller (1993) suggest that therapists need to attend to the spiritual belief systems of their clients in order to better understand them. They further contend that:

> Allowing the entrance of bias/subjectivity/spirituality into therapy has been construed by some as permitting the therapist to minimize, or ignore, the influence of his or her own values. Concepts such as hierarchy, boundaries, rules, patterns of interaction, and rigidity can be operationalized, quantified, and studied in an objective manner. However, subjective constructs (e.g., spiritual power, psychic energy, and divine intervention) are harder to observe and measure. (Prest & Keller, 1993, p. 139)

It is intriguing to note the mystical overtone given to constructs associated with spirituality, as if spirituality does not and could not exist in the concrete activities of daily living. Quoting James Bugental, one of the founders and leading theorists of the existentialist humanist psychology movement, Butler (1990, p. 30) writes,

> Spirituality is often misused. . . . It can be a cop-out, a way of not taking responsibility for one's life, for not confronting that we die, that what we do hurts those we don't want to hurt, that we don't live up to our own potential and our own values.

However, if, in fact, spirituality can be misused relative to concrete activities, it is equally reasonable that spirituality can be used appropriately, having a distinctive functional role in such areas as claiming responsibility, confronting death (in all its forms), and standing firm on values that help direct our lives.

Undoubtedly, a focus on spirituality is a double-edged sword. On the one hand, it is refreshing that therapists are entering a discussion about a level of reality that has meaning to many families. On the other hand, attention to deficiencies such as faulty beliefs (Prest & Keller, 1993), ill-training regarding concepts of God (Hanna, Myer, & Otters, 1994) and dysfunctional religious systems (Mac, 1994) is a small migration from ignoring spirituality entirely. To search for deficiencies does indeed pathologize spirituality, presenting it as a symptom of what's wrong and what needs to change. Beliefs, training and religious systems that contribute to family strength are rarely a focus of attention.

According to Jackson and Meadows (1991, p. 94), "culture is a connected living whole . . . [it is] alive, dynamic and all its elements are interconnected, each fulfilling a specific function in the integral scheme." Unfolding the components of deep culture involves examining underlying elements of philosophical assumptions inherent in ontology (what is real), cosmology (how does reality come to be and how does it change), epistemology (how we come to know what's real), axiology (what we value about what's real), logic (how we make sense of what's real) and process (how we function within our realities) (Jackson & Meadows, 1991). The ways in which family members talk with each other, spend time with each other, solve problems, raise children, nurture one another, forgive, love, trust, respect, and live with each other reflect the spiritual life of the family (Westbrooks, 1994). Spirituality is operationalized and personalized through roles, rules and patterns that are an inherent part of deep culture.

To understand deep culture is to address diversity at its roots—where and how we live. Although some attention has been paid to black families (Boyd-Franklin, 1989; Hill, 1972), ethnicity in families (McGoldrick, Pearce & Giordano, 1982), and unconventional strengths in families (Westbrooks, 1995), allegiance to standardized ways of judging and assessing has generally remained. Further attention to the role of culture, ethnicity and social class in a different kind of functional perspective have seemed to be marginal considerations at best. As Butler (1990, p. 33) notes,

> What shows up in a therapist's office as loneliness or purposelessness originates in a culture where people spend so much time commuting, working, or watching television that they have little left to develop what sociologist Robert Bellah calls "habits of the heart" with each other.

These habits of the heart may be understood as spiritual and involve connections and interconnections between the minds of family members and the larger community.

SPIRITUALITY AS A FORM OF FUNCTIONAL DIVERSITY

From a systems perspective we must be aware that our maps and our assessment metaphors or labels are not the territory (Becvar & Becvar, 1996, p. 321). A way of understanding healthy family functioning is no more than a map; it is an approximation describing characteristics of some families who are functioning normally in some circumstances. The traditional map, however, is heavily drawn from the experiences of one population group, effectively preserving ideas about the characteristics that define healthy functioning. To truly grapple with characteristics that do not fit our preconceived maps means to seriously consider changing the map. No one group should necessarily be a point of reference from which all families are judged and to which all families should aspire (Westbrooks, 1995).

However, as Fisher and Sprenkle (1978) noted nearly twenty years ago, constructs of "healthy" have virtually remained stable. Does this expectation of sameness persist even now as we head for the twenty-first century? Considering spirituality as a form of functional diversity means raising major questions about how spirituality influences or transforms our understandings of traditional constructs such as role performance (Lederer & Jackson, 1968; Liberman, 1972;), communication (Bateson, 1979; Haley, 1963; Satir, 1967; Whitaker, 1976), affective expression/involvement (Boszormenyi-Nagy, 1965; Bowen, 1978; Olson, Sprenkle & Russell, 1979), and control (Haley, 1963; Minuchin, 1974).

Thus to incorporate spirituality into a new understanding of family function means grappling with some of the basic assumptions of our traditional paradigm (Westbrooks, 1995). These assumptions may sound so familiar that to conceive of anything else seems unimaginable. However, the following ten generalizations are called into question by the anomaly (Kuhn, 1962) epitomized by many functional low-income families (Westbrooks, 1995).

1. Survival tactics and healthy family processes are not compatible. Assumptions about the incompatibility of survival tactics and healthy family processes reflect implicit ideas about unhealthy characteristics in low-income families. Ironically, voluminous research on poor families has contributed to a limited understanding of such families. We, in fact, have too many studies undertaken in the same way and with results interpreted in the same light. Generally research is done with the assumption that poor families, operating in survival mode, are dysfunctional social units and thus the focus of investigation is an assessment of the origin and patterns characterizing the dysfunction (Westbrooks, 1995, p. 18).

2. Role performance is dependent on clarity and specificity of task assignment. There is an assumption that role performance is dependent on clarity and specificity of task assignment which emerges from a cultural assumption that there must be one person "in charge." If the person in charge is clear and specific about what members are to do, when they are to do it and with whom, then roles will not be problematic and members will show responsibility. Within this cultural assumption, there is an implicit message regarding waiting to be told. In some cases, however, role performance is best actualized when there is "reliance on member ability to lead self and work collaboratively in regard to group goals" (Westbrooks, 1995, p. 128).

3. Communication is direct and open. The appropriateness of communication as direct and open depends on the situation. In some cases, being direct and open is appropriately curtailed by speaking to each other respectfully. Realizing that there is a time to speak and a time to be silent is a radical shift from there being only "one way." Communicating respectfully carries enormous meaning if family members have experienced a history of disrespect from the community at large. Respect for self and others is primarily shown through interactions and ways in which members send messages to each other. Communication is viewed as a means for feeling recognized, valued, affirmed and loved.

4. Expressions of affect are weak during times of stress. Skinner, Steinhauer and Santa-Barbara (1983) view the expression of affect as impeding or facilitating various aspects of task accomplishment and successful role integration. For those who embrace spirituality, bonding together during times of stress is precisely what helps them "get through the fire" and survive the heat. Affective expression may be a vital element in helping a family make it. Regardless of how intense things get, effort is made to preserve an expression of affect. During times of stress, affective expression is not blocked or distorted; in fact it is viewed as a strength (Westbrooks, 1995).

5. An aspect of affective involvement is trust. A traditional view of affective involvement includes the degree and quality of family members' interest in one another. Trusting is an acceptable factor of healthy affective involvement. However, what to trust and what not to trust are equally important for families who actively practice a form of spirituality. Thus caution is also introduced as a healthy characteristic.

6. Control involves the way members influence each other.

> Caution is the wisdom of knowing that you are not immune from dangers and set-backs. Therefore a degree of caution can initiate preparedness and shape skills that are useful in a context of dynamics that could threaten family well-being. (Westbrooks, 1995, p. 157)

In a traditional sense, control refers to the use of power and influence in interactions between members. The family is expected to be capable of successfully maintaining ongoing functions as well as adapting to shifting task demands. As many social workers know, "control is the process by which survival needs influence the way the family functions. Control has a dual focus of meeting basic needs and adhering to standards prescribed by the family" (Westbrooks, 1995, p. 108).

7. *Rules are flexible.* Ideas about rules being flexible are remnants of the time when professionals viewed some families as being much too rigid in terms of organization and structure. However, too much flexibility regarding rules can also be dysfunctional. According to Westbrooks (1995, p. 158), "rules that are more definite than flexible can be present in functional families, as evaluation shifts from an emphasis on a degree of rule flexibility to a focus on purpose and range of appropriateness of family rules."

8. *Latitude and scope is given for behaviors.* Latitude and scope have connotations similar to flexible rules. Ideas about giving members space to move freely are an accepted part of our traditional paradigm. However, "both latitude and limitation are elements in healthy behaviors; responsible latitude involves an awareness of responsible limits." Spirituality is an enormously key factor in the degree of freedom and limits that will be practiced within a family system. "Family values undergird the degree to which we are free and not free as values establish boundaries of behavior and also shape aspirations and goals" (Westbrooks, 1995, p. 160).

9. *Family values are consistent with the broader cultural context.* To have family values consistent with the broader cultural context assumes a cultural context that is family-friendly. According to Westbrooks (1995, p. 160-161),

> The societal context, which has long been considered the standard to which family values should aspire, has a developing role as contributing to family weakness. Growing societal dynamics, such as narcissism, accessibility of deadly drugs, gang warfare, homelessness, unemployment, apathy, and community violence are a few of many factors that threaten family well-being. A significant shift in the standard for family values is necessary if optimal family values are to survive. An emphasis on the spiritual life of a family rises above the functional or dysfunctional nature of a societal context and encourages us to consider an alternative, which focuses on spirituality as a measure and standard for family values.

10. *The territory for family processes is inside the family.* A focus on what is going on inside a family is traditionally viewed as the appropriate

territory for making judgments about family processes. For families who embrace spirituality, what is going on "outside" the family unit is also an appropriate focus of attention. The way a family is positioned in a social, economic, political and spiritual environment affects a family's perspective of what is supportive and what is threatening. Families who are respected, validated, sanctioned, accepted, and seemingly "protected" from societal ills may not be as aware of the external dynamics when they do not blatantly threaten family survival, identity, beliefs, and goals (Westbrooks, 1995).

Based on the above, we would suggest the following conclusions which call into question what previously have been considered as fundamental assumptions:

1. Survival tactics and healthy family processes are not necessarily contradictions.
2. Members are responsible not because they are assigned specific tasks, but because of an opportunity to show some initiative.
3. Communication involves a time to speak and a time to be silent.
4. Expressions of affect can be a strength during times of stress.
5. Affective involvement includes skills for discerning when to be either trusting or cautious.
6. Control includes family skills and responsibility for interpreting societal dynamics while building preparedness of members to constructively function in external systems.
7. Some rules are unchangeable and definite.
8. Behaviors have latitude within limits.
9. The societal context emerges as a potential threat to healthy family values; family values are consistent with the spiritual life of the family.
10. The territory for family processes involves both internal processes and external systems interaction.

A sense of balance, consistency and responsiveness reflects the nature of spirituality as evidenced in the above conclusions. To illustrate the role of spirituality in transforming some fundamental assumptions about the family, let us now briefly consider some findings regarding issues of survival, responsibility, communication, affective involvement, and rules. As regards survival,

> An integration of respect, love, faith in God, working together, and perseverance gives birth to an intriguing perspective on survival. There seemed to be silent consensus in the literature that there was an inherent aspect of the one way. (Westbrooks, 1995, p. 95)

Moral standards rooted in family spirituality may lead to a different way to survive and function. While largely untapped and unarticulated in a formal manner, delineating survival tactics may be extremely significant to our understanding of family processes in low-income families. Second, seeing responsibility as a function of the opportunity to show initiative has spiritual overtones because of issues regarding free will. A functional use of free will can help shape a sense of leadership and creativity. Third, the idea of a time to speak and a time to be silent is taken directly from the Holy Bible (Eccl. 3). Interpreting functional aspects of disclosure and non-disclosure depends on the nature of the relationship, lines of power and authority, rules regarding respect and boundaries regarding private matters. Fourth, to beware and stand ready are common themes within many religions. Indeed, families in the 1990's have reason to be cautious within an external context that is anti-family. Finally, there is the issue of whether it is possible for firm, strict, or more definite rules to have a functional role in family life. For example, family rules such as "practice self-respect and respect for others," "do not buy into someone else's definition of yourself (especially if that definition is negative)," and "never give up on constructive goals" are types that do not fit well into a category of flexibility. Rules have a "supposed to" quality. They govern and predict, answering such questions as, what are we to do, how should we do it, how soon should we do it, for what purpose and with whom? Functional family rules are meant to protect, guide and assist (Westbrooks, 1994).

Undoubtedly, spirituality is a lively integration of faith in action. It permeates family processes in ways that can be observable and in other ways that are beyond measure. It is the "breath of life" that awakens the heart and brings to a new level our understanding of roles, rules, and patterns.

FAITH AS AN UNCONVENTIONAL STRENGTH

"Functioning without the strokes of a societal community shapes strengths that are rooted in conviction rather than applause" (Westbrooks, 1995, p. 173). These strengths form a dynamic integration of characteristics that have roots in the spiritual life of family. Families interviewed in the study (Westbrooks, 1995) viewed faith as an essential tool for functioning within a context of different challenges. It is part of a collage of unconventional strengths that included defiance, survival and caution. Faith is an action tool that helps shape roles (doing), rules (guiding) and patterns (bonding). It embraces our very being and informs the distinctions we make between behaviors that are uplifting or denigrating, compassionate or critical, valuing or de-valuing.

ACTIVATING UNCONVENTIONAL STRENGTHS

When families list faith as one of their strengths, we are called to look for concrete ways in which it is a part of what works and what we can build on. If therapists assume that spiritual belief systems in families necessitate looking for what is wrong, we may unwittingly give a family a problem that they didn't have when they walked into our offices. Anderson and Worthen (1997) maintain that a therapist's degree of spirituality affects how she or he listens and responds throughout the session. Similarly, Mattson (1994) and Weaver, Koenig, and Larson (1997) note that evidence of the meaning and personal value of spirituality in families has called for needed discussion between clergy and family.

Activating this unconventional strength is helpful because it validates characteristics that may have emerged out of necessity. Accordingly, we convey a degree of value for families who have to function differently within a context of various challenges. We do not presume functional sameness nor do we presume that all families will use spirituality in the same ways. One way of activating faith as an unconventional strength is to find out from the clients for whom spirituality has value what they would like the people closest to them to remember as evidence of the Spirit of God at work in their lives or the evidence of faith in action. This may help clients isolate the role of faith in relationships, activities and experiences. When clients remember and can recount the ways that faith is real in their lives, what is activated is a renewed sense of spiritual endurance.

BUILDING ON SPIRITUAL SAMENESS TO CREATE CHANGE

There are times when faith and religious belief systems have a role in sustaining what is working for families. For this reason identifying what works and building on it is an essential part of the interventions articulated by many solution-focused approaches (e.g., Berg & De Jong, 1995). Roles, rules and rituals are means by which we personally integrate our faith. They are the channels through which our sense of values, love, and faith flow from one generation to the next. These may be characteristics that families seek to keep the same. Thus, it has been noted that family therapy and religion have interconnecting roles (Stander, Piercy, Mackinnon & Helmeke, p. 29) whose purposes are:

(a) to foster a sense of perspective,
(b) to give meaning to life,
(c) to provide rituals that transform and connect,
(d) to provide social support networks,

(e) to give an identity and heritage to its members,
(f) to support families,
(g) to facilitate positive change in individuals,
(h) to look out for the physical and emotional welfare of its members,
(i) to educate its members.

The viability of spirituality as a form of functional diversity calls us to examine the integral connections in roles, rules and patterns, directing our attention to questions about what works for whom, when and in what circumstances. For example, knowledge of who we are fosters a sense of perspective that is both within us and beyond us. The further we can reach back, the further we can reach forward into a future that retains meaning and value.

CONCLUSION

What has been proposed in this article is a call to seriously consider spirituality as a form of functional diversity. Examining active roles of faith in the concrete activities of daily living calls into question the once generally accepted scientific understanding of roles, rules, patterns, hierarchy, etc., as the only quantifiable, measurable and appropriate constructs. Expanding the boundaries of a boxed-in definition of spirituality presents a dual challenge. First, social workers and other therapists are challenged to consider spirituality as an aspect of deep culture that directs not only the way we interpret and make sense of what's real, but also how we participate in what's real. Roles, rules and patterns are in fact embedded in culture and reflect connections that are habits of the heart. The second challenge is to consider faith as an unconventional strength, thus activating faith to build on spiritual sameness to effect change. Perhaps both challenges are equally provocative. Certainly both call for a more balanced understanding of the role of spirituality in our work with families.

REFERENCES

Anderson, D., & Worthen, D (1997). Exploring a fourth dimension: Spirituality as a resource for the couple therapist. *Journal of Marital and Family Therapy*, *23*(1), 3-12.

Bateson, G. (1979). *Mind and nature*. New York: E. P. Dutton.

Becvar, D., & Becvar, R. (1996). *Family therapy. A systemic integration*, 3rd ed. Boston: Allyn & Bacon.

Berg, I. K., & De Jong, P. (1995). How to interview for client strengths and solutions. Unpublished Manuscript.

Boszormenyi-Nagy, I., & Framo, J. (Eds.) (1965). *Intensive family therapy: Theoretical and practical aspects.* New York: Harper and Row.

Bowen, M. (1978). *Family therapy in clinical practice.* New York: Jason Aronson.

Boyd-Franklin, N. (1989). *Black families in therapy: A multi-systems approach.* New York: The Guilford Press.

Butler, K. (1990). Spirituality reconsidered. *Family Therapy Networker, 14*(5), 26-37.

Fisher, B. L., & Sprenkle, D. H. (1978). Therapists' perceptions of healthy family functioning. *International Journal of Family Counseling, 6*(2), 9-18.

Haley, J. (1963). *Strategies of psychotherapy.* New York: Grune and Stratton.

Hanna, H., Meyer, R., & Otters, A. (1994). The effects of early religious training: Implications for counseling and development. *Counseling and Values, 39*(1), 32-41.

Hill, R. (1972). *The strengths of black families.* New York: Emerson Hall Publishers.

Jackson, A., & Meadows, F. (1991). Getting to the bottom to reach the top. *Journal of Counseling & Development, 70,* 72-76.

Kuhn, T. (1962). *The structure of scientific revolutions.* Chicago: University of Chicago Press.

Lederer, W., & Jackson, D. (1968). *The mirages of marriage.* New York: Norton.

Liberman, R. (1972). Behavioral approaches to family and couple therapy. In C. J. Sager & H. S. Kaplan (Eds.), *Progress in group and family therapy* (pp. 329-345). New York:Brunner/Mazel.

Mac, M. (1994). Understanding spirituality in counseling psychology: Considerations for research, training and practice. *Counseling and Values, 39*(1), 15-31.

Mattson, D. (1994). Religious counseling: To be used, not feared. *Counseling and Values, 38*(3), 187-192.

McGoldrick, M., Pearce, K. K., & Giordana, J. (1982). *Ethnicity and family therapy.* New York: Guilford Press.

Minuchin, S. (1974). *Families and family therapy.* Cambridge, MA: Harvard University Press.

Olson, D. H., Sprenkle, D. H., & Russell, C. S. (1979). Circumplex model of marital and family systems, and clinical applications. *Family Process, 18,* 3-28.

Prest, L. A., & Keller, J. F. (1993). Spirituality and family therapy: Spirituality beliefs, myths, and metaphors. *Journal of Marital and Family Therapy, 19*(2), 137-148.

Satir, V. (1967). *Conjoint family therapy.* Palo Alto: Science and Behavior Books.

Skinner, H., Steinhauer, P., & Santa-Barbara, J. (1983). The family assessment measure. *Canadian Journal of Community Mental Health, 2*(2), 91-105.

Stander, V., Piercy, F., Mackinnon, D., & Helmeke, K. (1994). Spirituality, religion, family therapy: Competing or complementary worlds? *The American Journal of Family Therapy, 22*(1), 27-41.

Weaver, A., Koenig, H., & Larson, D. (1997). Marriage and family therapists and the clergy: A need for clinical collaboration, training and research. *Journal of Marital and Family Therapy, 23*(1), 13-25.

Westbrooks, K. (1995). *Functional low-income families: Activating strengths.* New York: Vantage Press.

Westbrooks, K. (1994). *Overcoming dysfunction.* St. Louis: Concordia Publishing Houses.

Whitaker, C.A. (1976). The hindrance of theory in clinical work. In P. J. Guerin (Ed.), *Family therapy, theory and practice* (pp. 154-164). New York: Gardner Press.

The Spiritual Reality:
A Christian World View

Donald R. Bardill, PhD

SUMMARY. Every human being must answer the question, does God exist? If the answer is no, God does not exist, the follow-up question is, where or how will I anchor myself in *life*? If the answer is yes, God exists, the follow-up question must be, what is God's nature? To acknowledge that God exists and not seek God's nature is to ignore that which we ourselves believe created and rules the universe. The Christian World View addresses the nature of God from a very specific perspective. It is a perspective that organizes the lives of many of our clients. In this article the author presents a non-theological summary of the Christian spiritual perspective and relates some of the main Christian beliefs to family systems thinking as well as to implications for practice. *[Article copies available for a fee from The Haworth Document Delivery Service: 1-800-342-9678. E-mail address: getinfo@haworth.com]*

The Relational Systems Model (RSM)[1] posits that everything that exists in the realm of human relationships may be viewed within a circle of life realities that include self, other, context and spiritual. In RSM, reality is defined as what is. Of the four realities in RSM, three (self, other and context) are referred to as human realities and the fourth is the spiritual reality. The primary purpose of this discussion is to examine the spiritual reality from the Christian world view.[2] Within the framework of RSM,

Donald R. Bardill is Professor, School of Social Work, Florida State University, Tallahassee, FL 32306.

[Haworth co-indexing entry note]: "The Spiritual Reality: A Christian World View." Bardill, Donald R. Co-published simultaneously in *Journal of Family Social Work* (The Haworth Press, Inc.) Vol. 2, No. 4, 1997, pp. 89-100; and: *The Family, Spirituality and Social Work* (ed: Dorothy S. Becvar) The Haworth Press, Inc., 1998, pp. 89-100. Single or multiple copies of this article are available for a fee from The Haworth Document Delivery Service [1-800-342-9678, 9:00 a.m. - 5:00 p.m. (EST). E-mail address: getinfo@haworth.com].

89

attention will be given to a non-theological summary of some of the basic beliefs of the Christian spiritual perspective, chosen for discussion here because it is the world view with which the author is most familiar. Also, a substantial number of clients who seek family therapy in our country organize their lives around Christian spiritual beliefs. Some understanding of the basic belief system of Christian clients should help the social worker more easily join with these clients. Given the power of the spiritual reality in the lives of many of our clients, it is important that clinicians be prepared to evaluate the nature and place of clients' spiritual belief system as part of the overall assessment process.

THE REALITIES

The SOCSp triangle depicted in Figure 1 provides a way to visualize the four life realities, or self, other, context, spiritual. The inner triangle, composed of the three human realities, is surrounded by the spiritual reality. The manner in which all four realities are accounted for by individuals and aggregates of individuals forms the basis for the patterned human experience of their lives. For example, a person who habitually diminishes the reality of self will approach and experience life much differently than someone who habitually diminishes the reality of other people. All human experiences reflect the nature of a person's connection to, or lack of connection to, one or more life realities. Part of our individual uniqueness comes from the personal way we habitually connect to each life reality.

The Human Realities: Self, Other, Context

The reality of *self* is not easy to explain, yet as humans we are aware of our existence. We are "what is." We think, feel, see, and hear. We have an awareness of our place in the scheme of life. Self is my personal context, my essence. Self is the place from which I connect to all of life. Our awareness of ourselves means that we are conscious beings who not only know about existence, but know that we know. We are self-conscious beings. Self is the unique me.

From the Christian world view, our essential self includes a soul that lives forever. From this perspective, our body is the house in which the soul resides on this earth. Eternal life with God awaits those who are faithful to Jesus Christ.

The self may be thought of as the personal context for life. As a context for life, self contains the screen of life but never appears on it. The process of life imposes a set of tasks on the self reality. A critical life process for

FIGURE 1. SOCSp Triangle

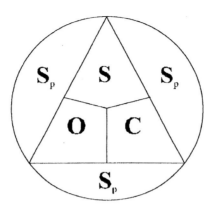

self involves the distinction between the self as the creator and the self as the created. In the realm of human realities the self creates and/or co-creates certain positions such as values, beliefs, identities, priorities, ideologies, and traditions. We tend to get attached and committed to these human creations. One of the sources of human dysfunction is found in the mistaken view that we *are* our views, values, beliefs, identities, etc. Therefore, any negative questions about our human-made creations become a threat to our sense of self. The failure to maintain distinctions between the self and the creations of the self is the arena for much of family therapy.

The other vital distinction for the self is the difference between the human as the created work of God and the reality of God. In our relationship to the spiritual reality we are the created and not the creator. We are finite beings whose essence includes a yearning to reconnect to our creator. At the same time, human history reveals a strong human inclination to create our own icons, or "Gods," to whom we can connect and devote our survival efforts. Our basic human nature includes a strong tendency to pursue our own personal desires and pleasures. Humans have the capacity to make narcissistic goals a kind of self-made god that in turn replaces God in their life. In a strange irony we end up being controlled by our own creations.

The *other* reality is everything organic and inorganic in the universe. Included in this reality are other human beings who exist in our experience. I am an other for you. You are an other for me. As a reality each self is required to account for other people in some way. Other people are the source of both pain and pleasure for us. We are connected to other human beings in various and complex sets of relationships. We relate to other people as individuals and in a wide range of aggregates such as the family or neighborhood.

As humans we are relationship dependent. The development of our personal patterned way of living is associated with our varying forms of human relationships. We have connections with other people. The very continuation and growth of the human race is founded on the intimacy of a commitment of an adult male and an adult female to each other and to the care of their children. All human beings are required to deal with emotional and social needs both for separateness and aloneness and for closeness and togetherness with others. We compete with each other for emotional and material resources and we need and want the closeness of others. A measure of human emotional maturity may be thought of as the ability to maintain a distinct self *and* be in a close relationship with others. Indeed, the maturity measure of marriage comes from the question, do I have the capacity to maintain a distinct self and be in a close intimate relationship with my spouse?

Context is everything that exists in the objective sense. It is the reality that is created by human beings through culture, society, bureaucracy, communities, religion, family, etc. It is a "made up" reality that we humans create through the various social systems that have evolved.

The contextual reality is powerful in that it creates a frame of reference against which we make meaning out of events. Our social communications with others are context dependent. The same words may have one meaning in one context and another meaning in a different context. For example, the word "ring" means one thing in the context of a signal to answer a telephone and yet have an entirely different meaning in the context of a wedding ceremony. The power of reframes in therapy comes from the importance of context in making meaning out of relational events. The process of assisting clients to see relationships and events from different perspectives is the basis of much of our clinical work.

The Fourth Reality: Spirit

The fourth, or *spiritual*, reality differs from the first three in that it refers to the existence of a transcendent creator or ruler of the universe, God. The spiritual reality may be thought of as the ultimate meaning-maker for all that exists.

The human sense of a spiritual reality is present in all known cultures. Surveys taken in the United States year after year have found that over 90 percent of the population believe in God. At the same time, the spiritual reality is subject to great misunderstanding, especially when the distinction between the spiritual and religion is not made clear. The spiritual reality, when subject to the forms of institutional religion, becomes part of the context reality. The spiritual reality and religion are not the same. Religion serves as a human made overlay or screen over the spiritual reality.

A FUNDAMENTAL QUESTION

The spiritual reality raises a fundamental question for each human being. The question is simple and complex. The question is, does God exist? If the answer is no, God does not exist, the follow-up question is where and how will I anchor myself in this life? Left to our own devices we humans create a set of moral rights or wrongs complete with values, beliefs and priorities that reflect a moral position. But, without God, from what source will we get the morals, ethics, rules to guide the path of conduct for humankind? The question of moral right and wrong cannot not be addressed.

The task of composing a fundamental world view for humans is a daunting one. It is not easy to create a reasonable human code of conduct and priorities without guidance from God. A Godless code of social conduct rests on the belief that there is no absolute moral truth except the absolute truth that there is no absolute truth. The "oughts" and "shoulds" of a social code of conduct created by humans will, at best, have to be based on human knowledge and desires. Science and materialism seem to be the most recent basis for our culture's moral and ethical positions. The vehicle for the content and process of the human-made code of social conduct will be the laws of society and the enforcement of those laws will be carried out by human beings.

In the worst case scenario, human conduct and priorities are based on the power plays of aggregates of people who have the resources to impose their own demands on others. Hitler is a classic example of the raw use of power to set the moral code for a society. In our own country the power of the media–television, movies, newspapers, books, etc.–to cleverly set the moral codes for people has become blatantly obvious. Morals by the media may become the basis for our evolving moral priorities and conduct.

For those who say there is no God, the world often becomes a have, an experience of do = be. In a have, do = be world view, what *I am* is a result of accumulations of such factors as power, money, prestige, etc., and the things I have done such as writing books, running a company, providing medical care, etc., in order to be a success or be happy. It's a world of doing, accomplishments and having in order to *be* something. The bumper sticker that says, "the winner is the one with the most toys" captures the driving force behind the have/do life perspective.

If the answer to the fundamental question, does God exist, is yes, the follow-up question is, what is God's nature? To acknowledge that God exists and not seek God's nature is to ignore that which we ourselves believe has created and rules the universe. A human being would be a strange creature indeed to know in his/her mind and heart that there is a creator of the universe and not seek to live in harmony with the creator.

THE CHRISTIAN SPIRITUAL REALITY

History shows that the search to understand the nature of God has gone in many directions. The Christian World View of God is a compelling perspective for many people. The essential message of the Holy Bible is the human struggle to relate to God within the dictates of a sin-prone human nature and God's never ending pursuit for a faith relationship with each and every human being. The dedicated Christian connects to the spiritual reality through an active faith relationship with Jesus Christ. For the Christian, the biblical God of Abraham, Isaac, Jacob and Moses in the Old Testament and that same God who revealed himself in Jesus Christ in the New Testament is the one true God; there is no other God. The Christian believes that the Holy Bible is the inspired living word of God. The Bible is God's self-disclosure about how he comes to us or is accessible to us. Thus, the Christian looks to the Bible for an understanding of the nature of God. The word of God as revealed in the Bible is easy to understand and it is not easy to understand. The Bible is a book of mystery with a both/and quality. It is a doctrine for only the most dedicated thinker and spiritual explorer and its essential message is understood by children. It has simplicity and it has depth. It demands both reason and faith. The Christian constantly uses the Bible in an unending search to learn about the unknowable nature of God. It is in this constant search for the truth that the mystery and power of God emerges. The process of seeking to know God brings God to us.

While finite humans will never completely know the infinite nature of God, the Bible consistently reveals some fundamental truths about our creator. In the Christian spiritual reality, all humans are created in God's love primarily to worship, praise and love God, and secondly, to love each other. In the spiritual scheme of life, God is primary and our relationship to him and to other people is to be a reflection of God's will. The Bible is clear about our relationship to God. God is God and we are his creations.

As humans we are autonomous beings who are limited only by the finiteness of our human nature. Within our human nature we have freedom of choice. As an autonomous being each of us is free to choose to live our life with or without a faith relationship to God. The choice to live life on earth without a relationship to God is a choice available to all humans. God does not force himself upon any human being. When we reject a relationship with God, we get exactly what we choose. Our choice is a choice for all eternity. Thus, for the Christian, the primary reality in life, and for eternity, is that he/she has received the gift of Jesus Christ as Lord and Savior. For the Christian, hell would be eternity without the presence of God's love.

In the Christian World View, the human being has eternal life. When a human dies on earth it is not the end of his/her existence. Eternal life with God is available through the faith relationship with Jesus Christ. Thus, created in the image of God to love and worship God, nothing but a relationship with Christ will satisfy the soul's yearning to connect to its creator.

For the Christian something happens to the human being when he/she is fully connected to God. The power of the creator of the universe is activated in his/her life. A sense of wholeness and abundance becomes part of human existence on earth. The Christian's yearning to know about the nature of God and His will for humankind is part of a spiritual maturity process. The human *need* to pursue personal glory and power subsides as the Christian grows in his/her closeness to God. However, to say that the need to acquire personal power or possessiveness diminishes does not imply that a Christian does not, or cannot, enjoy earthly success. The essential point is that he/she does not need such things for a sense of well-being. Power and possessions may be enjoyed but they do not rule the Christian's life. The maturing Christian knows that a personal sense of "OK-ness" is a by-product of seeking God and His will in life. Happiness, excitement and serenity all are the outflowing, the effect, of connecting to God's love.

Thus, the maturity process for the Christian is a constant state of becoming "what I am" as a child of God. It's a constant process of doing what fits for who and what I am. The motivation for growth and change comes from the process of saying "yes" to Christ. The goal in life is to live out my beingness in Christ.

Will Christians have problems on this earth? The answer is yes! Indeed, many problems experienced by a Christian may come from the fact of being a Christian. However, for the true believer in Christ, problems take on a different meaning. God promises that all things work for the good of people who love Him. Christians live in the freedom of the love commandment (love God with all your heart, mind and soul and love your neighbor as yourself) and the ten commandments. This means that Christians are free to love people rather than attack them, to worship God above all else, to not kill, to honor their family members, to be faithful to their spouses, to enjoy a day of rest and worship in every week, to not be controlled by the economic rat-race (the winner in a rat-race is still a rat), to find satisfaction in our life's possessions, and finally, to enjoy the lifestyle of our neighbors (there is no need to be driven to keep up with the culture's thundering social and economic herds). A Christian is free, free to be who and what he/she is in his/her relationship to God.

Christians, like all human beings, have trouble harnessing a part of their nature. Referred to in the Bible as "the old Adam in us," humans are inclined to disobey God's will and, even worse, attempt to deny their disobedience. God says that people who love Him keep His commandments. Thus, through our disobedience to God we daily break our relationship with Him. We put our own desires first. Disobedience is totally unacceptable to God.

In our "old Adam," it is impossible to live in harmony with God. The experience of Adam and Eve in the Garden of Eden tells us that as humans, and without God's help, we are incapable of either obeying God's will or recognizing and owning our disobedience.[3] However, God understands the human proclivity toward disobedience. It is at this point of God's love and understanding and the human inability to obey Him, that God provides a way to reconnect to Him. That is, in his enormous love for each and every human being, God sent his son, Jesus Christ, to earth to suffer and to die on a cross for our disobedience. Jesus arose from the dead for every human being. In the death and resurrection of part of himself, God atoned for the mistakes of all humankind. In the Christian spiritual reality, all past errors of disobedience have been forgotten for those who truly believe in God through Jesus Christ. Salvation from our sins is a gift to us from God.

While a human being cannot of his/her own will *do* enough to earn a place in eternity with God, an openness to receiving Christ as God and savior of the world says to God, "Here I am, I give up my old self as primary in life. I confess my past errors and mistakes, come and get me as your own." In that moment of confession and by saying, "I give up. I can't do it, I need you God," the hand of God reaches down to me and a reconnection to God takes place; an eternal relationship has been formed.

In the frame of RSM, putting God first is a process of making the human realities secondary to the enormity of the spiritual reality. The fundamental Christian World View says that when I fully acknowledge my errors and mistakes against God and other people by owning them and confessing them to God, my relationship to God and other people is strengthened and enhanced. God wipes my past mistakes and errors away forever.

Even the most casual observer will notice that God does not take our personality, our uniqueness, away from us as a condition for our relationship to Him. Christians present themselves in all personality types. The vital fact for the Christian is the constant effort to live his/her life in a close faith relationship to Jesus Christ and his love. When the Christian falls short in pleasing God, forgiveness is sought, and God's love reaches out to him/her in forgiving grace. The God of the universe says to the believer, you are OK! However, Christ's love is never the basis for violent destructive behavior. If any action is not in love, it is not based in Christ. It is based in some other process. The essence of Christ is love and all that is of God spins out of *that* specific reality.

Finally, a discussion of the Christian World View would be incomplete without acknowledging that the designation "Christian" has a variety of meanings. For some people in our country, a Christian is someone who is an extreme right wing political operative; a very negative picture of Christianity. For other people, a Christian is a person who centers his/her life in the love of God; a positive response to the notion of a "Christian." Given the powerful feelings, both negative and positive, that many people hold toward Christians, every social worker will need to examine his/her own particular inner pictures of what "Christian" means. Managing our own personal biases toward any particular client group is foundational to professional ethics.

Beginning where the client is has always been a fundamental value in social work. That means that we do not attack a client's unique connection to the spiritual reality, nor do we seek to impose our own spiritual reality on the client. A discerning social worker will assess both the importance and the specific nature of the spiritual reality in the life of his/her client. To learn that a client is a "Christian" offers only a vague picture about what his/her basic belief system may be. Christians themselves hold a variety of beliefs about what it means to be a "Christian."

DISCUSSION

The Christian World View is in harmony with many of the basic principles of systems-based family work. For example, the self-differentiation (Bowen, 1978) process pushes me to work for a solid self that knows who and what I am and to live my life in congruence with my essential self. Being a Christian provides a basis for me to live my life in congruence with my essential self. The capacity to remain non-anxious in threatening situations is rooted in a solid sense of self that (1) knows the difference between emotions and thinking and strives to make room for emotion while keeping the thinking process in charge of responses; (2) maintains a balance between the push to be both a unique, separate individual and together with other people; and (3) has the ability to make distinctions between the Creator and the created. We are God's creations and we live within the universal context of a transcendent reality. We also create internal realities (values, beliefs, identities, etc.) that in turn govern how we make meaning of life.

The human struggle to manage our basic survival anxieties is universal. In our anxiety we intrude on the boundaries of others through either our dependency or our attacks against them. The reality is that we are interconnected with each other and we are unique individuals. Our lower self, expressed through our survival fears, is easily frightened. The ongoing struggle to allow emotional expression while approaching life in thoughtful, reflective ways is a basic part of the human condition. For the Christian, knowing who and what I am in Christ provides a place on which to stand in life–and eternity.

The process of self-examination that results in ownership of our actions for the purpose of growth reminds me of God's command both to confess our sins to him so that he might forgive us and the basic human need for self awareness about destructive and growth behaviors. Both self awareness and confession require a safe place. Being in the presence of God is a safe place and, at its best, the therapeutic atmosphere is a place of safety and trust. The yearning for a place of quiet comfort and acceptance is a part of human nature. The therapist who listens to the client story in a nonjudgemental manner and with genuine respect co-creates a context for trust and caring. Someone once described paradise as a place where everyone is speaking and hearing in the same caring language.

The commandment first to love God and second to love each other addresses the never ending boundary issues between and among people and between human beings and God. Clearly, humans thrive best in their uniqueness *and* in a close relationship to God and to each other. The Christian God is a God of unconditional love for those who are in a relationship with Him. In love, each person is free to be a unique self and to be in relationships with others. An outcome of all family counseling is each family member's increased capacity to stand on his/her own two feet and be in a close, caring family group.

The process of maintaining the distinction between the creator and created is a struggle that never ends for the human being. Knowing that I am God's creation does not keep me from making my own personal rules and priorities, many of which contradict God's will. Knowing that I created and/or co-created certain values, beliefs, identities, etc., does not keep me from defending them as if they form my very essence. When my human-made priorities and identities are attacked, I mistakenly react as if my very survival is threatened. The process of recognizing human-made priorities and identities is facilitated by the process of externalization of values and beliefs so that it is possible to view them in a more dispassionate frame of reference.

CONCLUSION

The relational systems model pushes for an examination of connections to all four of the life realities. RSM does not demand specific content for facing the realities but it does encourage close attention to the process by which each reality is accounted for in all our relationships. The core of effective family work will almost always involve some version of the multi-dimensional[4] "facing process." This means a careful examination of any discrepancy between who and what I say I am and what I do and seek to accumulate, or have, in my life. The facing process is not easy. It includes a detailed inner-look at my overall purpose in life. It is well to remember that purpose is a context provider and, as such, is a direction given and a meaning-maker. For some people, the primary source of their direction in life comes from either the wider society, unmanaged inner fears and desires, or parts of both. It is as if we have given all our power of self-hood to something smaller than our essence. For some of us the primary source for direction in life comes from a growing connection to Jesus Christ. For clients who make a strong connection to the spiritual, it often is helpful to explore the effects of their spiritual connection on their life.

The second task in the facing process is a truthful look at what we actually *do* and how we actually construct our world view; how we language our experiences and what material and power accumulations we *have* in our life, all of which are accurate reflections of our guiding purpose in life. In terms of responsibility, it is a process of owning exactly what is mine to own (values, priorities, actions, beliefs, etc.). It may well be that the degree of discrepancy between what we do and have *and* who and what we say we are is a measure of the dysfunction in our life. The process of examining what I know and how I know it is an extremely powerful force in the search to connect to the realities of life. It is only when I take ownership of who and what I am and what I do and have that the possibility for change emerges. In our fearfulness, we constantly accuse (blame) others or context, excuse (deny), or both, any perceived mistakes. In our growth, we connect to ourself and the whole of life. We own that which is ours to own, nothing more, nothing less. Simply stated, the facing process means that we get honest with ourselves. The act of self-responsibility will create change in our life.

Third, for the dedicated Christian, the facing process inevitably will involve the story of the client's ongoing quest to know the nature of God. The story will be told only if the client senses that the therapist wants to hear and will respect the story. The nature of the client's connection to the spiritual reality will bring wholeness to the personal world view.

Finally, a point of vital importance is that the congruence between the Christian World View and the process of RSM-oriented family systems work can be of enormous help to the therapy process. The orientation to wholeness, growth and abundance characterizes both perspectives. The recognition of the existence of the four life realities makes attention to all of the realities a vital part of the therapy process. The opportunity to tap into the foundational place on which a client stands, and to use that source to promote client growth, is one that social workers need not miss.

NOTES

1. See Bardill, D., *The Relational Systems Model: Living in the Four Realities* (1997), Binghampton, NY: The Haworth Press, Inc.

2. The author is fully aware of spiritual world views other than the Christian perspective. In the process of working with clients their spiritual reality may be expressed in many ways.

3. See Genesis, Chapter 3 of the Holy Bible. The most destructive part of the story of Adam and Eve in the Garden of Eden is not that they disobeyed God by eating the forbidden fruit but that they tried to hide what they had done by denying responsibility for their actions.

4. See pp. 234-253 in *Relational Systems Model for Family Therapy: Living in the Four Realities* (1997) Binghamton, NY: The Haworth Press, Inc.

REFERENCES

Bardill, D. R. (1997). *The Relational Systems Model for Family Therapy: Living in the Four Realities*. Binghamton, NY: The Haworth Press, Inc.

Bowen, M. (1978). *Family therapy in clinical practice*. New York: Jason Aronson.

New American Standard Bible. (1977). Nashville, TN: Thomas Nelson Publishers.

Giving Good Sermons in Therapy

Thomas Edward Smith, PhD
Pamela V. Valentine, PhD
Rebecca Martin Williams, MDiv

SUMMARY. Social workers and other therapists often deliver "sermons" which are not heard by their clients. Like some preachers who lose their congregations with dull monologues, therapists can lose their audiences through ineffective preparation or poor delivery. The effective preparation and delivery of messages are addressed in the body of literature known as homiletics. This article begins a conversation between practitioners of homiletics and of family therapy. A discussion of the vital elements of an effective sermon as well as its preparation and delivery that makes sense to clients is offered. Vignettes to illustrate various uses of sermons in therapy are included. *[Article copies available for a fee from The Haworth Document Delivery Service: 1-800-342-9678. E-mail address: getinfo@haworth.com]*

A sermon is like a brick; it fulfills its function only as it is placed in relationship in a structure. (Perry, 1993, p. 3)

INTRODUCTION

Social workers and other therapists routinely offer sermons: messages, interventions, or advice to clients in the form of one-liners or longer

---

Thomas Edward Smith is Professor of Social Work, Florida State University, Tallahassee, FL. Pamela V. Valentine is Assistant Professor of Social Work, University of Alabama-Birmingham, Birmingham, AL 35294. Rebecca Martin Williams is a doctoral candidate in practical theology at the Union Theological Seminary in Virginia.

Address correspondence to: Thomas Edward Smith, School of Social Work, Florida State University, Tallahassee, FL 32306-2024 (E-mail: tsmith@mailer.fsu.edu).

[Haworth co-indexing entry note]: "Giving Good Sermons in Therapy." Smith, Thomas Edward, Pamela V. Valentine, and Rebecca Martin Williams. Co-published simultaneously in *Journal of Family Social Work* (The Haworth Press, Inc.) Vol. 2, No. 4, 1997, pp. 101-113; and: *The Family, Spirituality and Social Work* (ed: Dorothy S. Becvar) The Haworth Press, Inc., 1998, pp. 101-113. Single or multiple copies of this article are available for a fee from The Haworth Document Delivery Service [1-800-342-9678, 9:00 a.m. - 5:00 p.m. (EST). E-mail address: getinfo@haworth.com].

soliloquies (Smith & Counsell, 1991). However, as noted by the family therapy supervisor to the student therapist who was rambling about the "right thing to do" to two young clients, "I don't think your preaching is getting through to them." The clients, of course, were not listening.

Preaching has often been equated with dull monologues filled with predictable platitudes that many people instinctively learn to disregard. Unfortunately, the negative characterization of sermons may have prevented clergy and secular therapists from taking advantage of an entire body of literature that studies the effective preparation and delivery of messages: Homiletics. This article therefore begins a conversation between practitioners of homiletics and of family therapy. The conversation includes two central themes. First, both secular and religiously-minded therapists can benefit from techniques developed within the field of homiletics. Second, religiously-minded and non-religiously-minded clients can be positively affected by these techniques, since the sermon is prepared and delivered to fit clients' world views. To better understand the relationship between homiletics and family therapy, the discussion is organized into two broad areas: elements of a good sermon and tips for preparing sermons that make sense to the client. We also have included vignettes throughout the article to give examples of our assertions.

Before we begin the discussion of the elements of a good sermon, a few comments on the therapy vignettes are in order. Those used to illustrate different sermon elements are distinctively Christian in nature. However, the intent is not to suggest that all good sermons must be Christian sermons. Religious content should be respectful of the client's language/culture/symbols and religious orientation. Second, the use of religious language might not be an effective choice for nonreligious clients, yet it may be required for those whose world view is colored by religious ideology. Ignoring religiously-minded clients' language renders many sermons as impotent as sermons filled with "God-talk" would be when addressed to atheists. Finally, good sermons are notable in their multiple qualities and missions: they instruct, inspire, reframe, surprise, evoke, and mesmerize clients. These qualities and missions are discussed and illustrated below.

ELEMENTS OF A GOOD SERMON

1. Good sermons are instructional; they often extend a person's understanding of the world by hinting at answers to perplexing questions about pain. People are naturally curious about why events occur, especially trying events that have affected their lives. Explanations of phenomena appeal to clients and can ease the grief and anxiety of trauma.

Vignette #1

A woman presented for therapy due to a series of family problems that had weighed her down for years. She stated that she was a Christian who lived an "examined," responsible life. As a result, she expected to "reap good things." Her adherence to the principle of sowing and reaping led her to believe that her troubles were somehow her fault. Not seeing a link between her behavior and life's painful events, the therapist delivered a sermon pertaining to the Last Supper that Jesus had with his disciples: "And he took the bread, and gave thanks, and brake it, and gave it unto them . . . " (Luke 22:19). The therapist told her that as Jesus had done with the bread, so he does with our lives. He takes us, blesses us, breaks us (i.e., humbles us and causes us to be dependent on God), and finally, He shares us with others. Only after breaking us are we suitable for His purposes. With this explanation, the woman began feeling privileged rather than persecuted by her trials. She could surrender to the mysterious process in hopes of a better end.

2. A sermon must have inspirational qualities (i.e., "It touches a person's soul"). Inspiration is difficult to define, but intrinsically it involves "the power of moving the intellect or emotions" (Miriam-Webster, 1993); it is an artistic phenomenon (cf., Papp, 1984). In short, the inspirational quality of a sermon both comments on and influences a person's existential questions. By reaffirming positive values (i.e., positive to the person who is listening), good sermons inspire. This does not mean that sermons only reaffirm existing positive values. A good sermon can also convince listeners of the virtue of new values that were previously not highly regarded. By moving the intellect or the heart, the sermon has inspired clients.

Vignette #2

A lesbian couple, Monica and Grace, presented in therapy to work on both individual and couple issues. Four months before the session, Monica's twin sister had died. Monica and Grace reported casually that Monica had wanted to kill herself the previous Saturday night. Asking further, the social worker learned that Monica was no longer suicidal because she had heard God tell her that He wanted her to have a baby *and to have it now.* Monica was very excited. The social worker asked Monica if she saw any incongruence in wanting to take her life Saturday night and wanting to give life Sunday. Monica did not. The social worker probed as to the mutuality of the decision. No red flags. Next the social worker asked

Monica's reasons for wanting a child. She spoke of how a child would love her most of the time and sought the social worker's reaction to her decision to bear a child. The social worker responded that she had two reactions: one from the secular world and one from the Scriptures. The secular world would advise you to not make any major decisions within a year of a traumatic event like your sister's death. And the Scriptures say, "For a thousand years in thy sight are but as yesterday when it is past, and as a watch in the night " (Psalms 90:4). We are often so excited when we hear God speak that we rush to do His will. In our haste, we don't realize that our timing may be different from that of God's. The Bible speaks of the long suffering nature of God. You might try the following: Tell God that you are eager to do His will, but ask Him to be patient with you. Since you want to be sure of His will, ask Him for the next year to remind you daily of His will. If, at the end of the year, you still hear Him say, "Have a baby," you'll have it. I'll bet that a year is like a blink of the eye to God.

The sermon blended elements of old values (belief in the Scriptures to guide one's life) with new values (waiting to have a baby, yet still feeling as if one is being obedient to God). The client felt inspired to try something different. Months later, about the time that therapy was ending, Monica told the social worker that the idea of a baby had arisen as a way to console herself regarding her sister's death.

3. Good sermons reframe (provide a new understanding to old problems [Minuchin & Fishman, 1981; Haley, 1976]). Using reframes in therapy is not new. What is suggested here, however, is that good sermons often contain this familiar element. The precedent for such elements in a sermon could be argued from Scripture itself. Capps (1990) suggests that throughout His ministry on earth, Jesus Christ was a master reframer. His sermons, such as the Beatitudes, capitalize on reversals: "Blessed are the meek, for they will inherit the earth" (Matthew 5:5). Then again, reframing the definition of "sinner," Jesus challenged a crowd intent on stoning an adulterous woman, saying, "Let anyone among you who is without sin be the first to throw a stone at her" (John 8:7b). This new understanding allows people flexibility in their world views. Maruyama (1977) calls this phenomenon a "polyocular view" of the world; others suggest that this method of construing the world represents a balance between constructivism and positivism called "perspectivism" (Breunlin, Schwartz, & Mac-Kune-Karrer, 1992). Clients are not needlessly constrained by any one way of thinking and thus are given the opportunity to apply graceful solutions to difficult problems. Good preachers as well as therapists employ reframes; they link together diverse elements in clients' lives so that a phenomenon may be perceived in a new manner.

Vignette #3

A middle-aged minister, depressed and burned-out after twelve years in the pastorate, acknowledged having spent countless hours trying to be "strong, happy, and righteous." Now he found himself somber and serious, having forgotten how to enjoy life. He was working part-time as a child-care provider in a day care center. The counselor asked him, "Do you enjoy your work?" To his own surprise, he responded, "Yes! Very much!" At the end of the session, a sermon was delivered on the theme of learning from children how to live. The sermon was based on a passage that the minister had remembered earlier in the session: "Truly I tell you, unless you change and become like children, you will never enter the kingdom of heaven. Whoever becomes humble like this child is the greatest. . . ." (Matthew 18:3-5). In the weeks that followed, the minister began to listen to what the children were teaching him about playing, laughing, sharing, and loving.

4. To have people attend to the message given, a sermon's content and delivery should be unpredictable in its challenges and reaffirmations. The old should be combined with the new. Similar to therapy, clients must be reassured while simultaneously being challenged. This can be done only if at times the message cannot be wholly predicted by the listener. Messages given repeatedly and predictably will eventually result in nonattendance by the listener. Perry (1993) explains that less effective sermons "elaborate on the obvious. This attempt to major on the minutia will short-circuit the attention span of the listener" (p. 4). Typically, "surprises" will, by contrast, both intrigue and reassure clients. The unpredictability in a message, in effect, makes the ideas interesting. Of course, if messages are too far removed from clients' experiences, they may be distracting and result in clients' disregarding the sermon.

Vignette #4

A basketball coach came to therapy to "understand his emotions," believing that so doing would benefit his relationship with his wife. However, he hurried from one topic to another, thus preventing the opportunity to know himself. The client focused on right and wrong to the point of categorizing emotions; for him, anger was a "wrong" emotion. A reframe was especially needed since the client neither wished to be "found wanting" nor wished to be angry. One day the client joyfully related a story about his having trusted God in a challenging financial situation. The social worker took a pleasant experience (i.e., trusting God) and broadened it by asking, "Why can you trust God with your finances, but not with your emotions?" This question surprised the client, yet he received the "call" to further trust God with his emotions, knowing that it was the right thing to do. Since that session, the client has experienced a range of emotions and feels that he is making progress in relating to his wife.

5. A vital component of sermons is an illustration (e.g., story, metaphor, symbol) that carries the power of the message beyond the words spoken. Illustrations should be limited to one per idea, remembering that "fresh, brief, and simple" is best (Perry, 1993, p. 83). Perry further argues that an effective illustration "will serve to illuminate the subject, hold attention, stimulate the imagination, aid the memory and make the message more practical" (1993, p. 83). Combs and Freedman (1990) offer a compelling discussion on the use of stories, metaphors and rituals in therapy, suggesting that the necessary interpretive dimension of such activities allows for client partnership and therapist flexibility. We echo their enthusiasm, pointing to the sermon as an important place for the inclusion of illustrations/imagery.

Vignette #5

A female client was lamenting the number of painful discoveries she was encountering in her work in therapy. Questioning the fairness of God, she asked, "How many 'bottoms' do I have to hit?" The social worker asked, "How many did Jesus have to hit?" "The cross," she responded. "I know it was terrible, but then it was over." The social worker delivered a sermon about the road to the cross. She reminded the client of Jesus sweating drops of blood, Peter's denying knowing Jesus, the spitting, the mockery, the whipping, the crown of thorns, carrying His own cross on a bloody back, seeing His mother weep for him, and finally, feeling God "forsake" Him. As the client visualized the road to the cross, she understood that each of the stages of the cross probably felt like a "bottom" to Jesus . . . like it could not get any worse. Standing apart from her problems, she saw the importance of partializing an event. Failing to partialize a current event makes it overwhelming; failing to partialize a past event makes it trivial. The story put the client's suffering in a new perspective for her and she felt encouraged to go forth and continue the work of therapy.

6. The sermon's delivery is as important or more important than the content. Voice intonation, cadence, emotion, and therapist body language should match the message. Although this may seem obvious, therapists often present themselves to clients in a manner that is incongruent with the message they intend to communicate. For example, an unaware therapist might walk energetically around the therapy room exhorting a couple in a loud, demanding voice that they relearn how to romance each other–a reasonable sermon, perhaps, but with a voice and manner that are antithetical to the message.

Effective sermons often have the hypnotic, highly cadenced, repetitive nature that will encourage a trance. The key here is that the repetitive nature of words and/or gestures should be purposeful and should not be mannerisms that distract clients. Support for conversational hypnotic inductions comes from the work of Milton Erickson and more recently from practitioners such as Steve and Carol Lankton (1986). An example of purposeful repetition can be found in Psalms 136 in which each of the 26 verses ends with, "for His mercy endureth forever." This use of repetition can help create a calm and reassuring ambiance, thus enabling the listener to be receptive to messages being given. A therapist who has first listened to the client now has earned the "right to be heard." This balance of powers helps make clients ready to receive such messages and/or directives, and the repetitive phrases are a "hook" that will hold their attention. This might mean, for example, that some mutually acceptable phrases should be used to hypnotically prepare clients for interventive messages.

The use of sermons in therapy may be interwoven with classic brief therapy interventions such as compliments and specific directives for change (de Shazer, Berg, Lipchik, Nunnally, Molnar, Gingerich, & Weiner-Davis, 1986). Compliments produce a "yes-set" that makes the clients amenable to directives for change (de Shazer et al., 1986). O'Hanlon and Weiner-Davis (1989) take advantage of mildly hypnotic suggestions in asking a "miracle question," an invitation for the client to visualize how his or her life will look after a miracle takes place and all is well. The following shows the entwining of brief therapy techniques and sermons.

Vignette #6

A young couple requested counseling for their troubled marriage as well as for the wife, who was convinced she had an anxiety disorder. The husband was a third year seminary student preparing for the pastorate in a fundamentalist church. Neither husband nor wife thought anything positive was occurring in their marriage, and the wife was beginning to believe her anxiety "disorder" might be of a permanent nature. The "miracle question" was asked within the religious context of their belief in a God of miracles. After each miracle scene was explored in detail and affirmed, the following sermon was offered:

> I imagine you are familiar with the passage in Isaiah: "God's thoughts are not our thoughts, neither are His ways our ways." So ask yourselves, "Are you willing for God to work changes in your lives in mysterious ways?" Next week don't try to change anything.

The message was intended to plant a suggestion that change could come unexpectedly, for their faith affirmed that mysterious events are as possible as ordinary events. It also was intended to create doubt about the "truth" gathered from books which suggested poor prognosis and inevitable long-term therapy for someone suffering from an anxiety disorder.

During the following week's session, the couple announced that pleasant changes had occurred for both. Questions were posed presupposing that changes had rippled into other areas of their lives as well, including their relationship with God. At the end of the session, the therapist preached a sermon entitled "Memory Stones" based on Joshua 2:4-24:

> After the people of Israel crossed the Jordan river, which had been parted by God, they were instructed by Joshua to collect stones from the center of the river and build a monument on the river bank. The collection of stones was to serve as a reminder for generations to come of this momentous occasion. God knew the human tendency to forget successes and dwell on problems. I believe God's advice to you would be the same today. Gather stones of these moments and fix them in your heart and memory, so that when leaner times come, you can return to the truth of these events and not be fooled by passing trials.

The point of the message was twofold. First, it reasserts that the couple had encountered a "river" to cross and had done so with God's help. Second, it predicts that "leaner times" will come, placing them in a context that normalizes problem recurrence and empowers them toward further resolution. Familiar postures of sermon delivery within the particular context of the faith of this couple were used: The delivery of the sermon included deliberate emphasis on command words such as "gather," "fix" and "return." There was also strong eye contact accompanied by a firm but gentle voice.

7. The ultimate test of a "good" sermon is its effectiveness. Homileticians want to know, "Did the audience resonate with the message?" "Did they respond with their eyes and ultimately, with action?" One of the authors of this article remembers her first experience in preaching. She had arrived in the midst of a small rural congregation, prepared to deliver her "one-sermon-fits-all" message without particular attention to the language and values of the congregation's culture. Her greatest clue that her message had missed its mark was when a well-meaning older member, upon exiting, passed her and shook hands with her husband, thanking him for the message! The congregation's failure to remember her or her sermon within minutes of its delivery highlighted the failure to tailor the message to the audience.

A growing number of homileticians are concerned with holding the attention of their audiences. The idea is that even a brilliant sermon will fall on deaf ears if the intended listeners speak different languages or appeal to different traditions. Such a statement may seem obvious, yet homileticians complain that it rarely is taken seriously in churches or, for that matter, in therapy rooms. When cultures are visibly diverse, therapists may well attend to the need to tailor their message and delivery to their audience. However, without such visible clues as, for example, ethnicity, therapists may assume greater homogeneity than exists.

Smith and Counsell (1991) approach the topic by advising that therapists not assume they understand the particular religious language of their clients. Preferably, non-clergy social workers should wait until the clients themselves identify scripture and religion as their frame of reference. Then, they might ask clients to help them understand the role of God (the Church, the Scriptures, etc.) in their lives. For example, "How does your faith address your problem? What does it say about forgiveness, hardships, joy, etc.?" If the client is unsure, but interested, the therapist might utilize homework assignments to search for such answers: "Look in the Gospels for conditions where Christ was helpful when no one else was."

TOWARD GOOD SERMONS THAT MAKE SENSE
TO THE CLIENT

Social workers can adopt two stances that will help them give good sermons: therapists as ethnographer and as "hearer." Regarding the former stance, in *Preaching as Local Theology*, Tisdale (1992) suggests that becoming an ethnographer is the first step toward effective preaching. Using anthropological literature, she argues for a semiotic analysis of the intended hearer's subculture as a crucial component of sermon preparation. This approach is concerned with the symbolic dimensions of a culture (e.g., signs, symbols, signifiers) which create systems of meaning within a society. Schreiter (1986) explains that the task of semiotics is "to describe and explain the signs, their interaction, the rules that govern them, and the complex that we call culture which emerges from all of this" (p. 50).

However, Clifford Geertz (1973) reminds us that variability in interpretations of signs and symbols means that cultures (client systems and subsystems) can be described in a variety of ways, most of which are equally valid. Further, the interpretations we offer are always only "particular," not "privileged" (p. 23). Thus, Geertz argues, a semiotic approach does not attempt to discover some static entity (e.g., a diagnostic criterion) but aims toward "gaining access to the conceptual world in which our subjects live so that we can, in some extended sense of the term, converse with them" (p. 24).

The argument here is simple: A semiotic analysis of a client system will suggest avenues for effective sermon writing and delivery. However, the point is not that therapists should engage in formal ethnographic studies of each client system. They should, however, employ careful observation (which many therapists are already doing) as useful, required resources to guide effective message preparation and delivery. It is in this arena that therapists become familiar with what role signs and symbols play in a client's world and what they mean to the client. Many a "good" sermon delivered by well-meaning therapists has been known to fail–or fall short of its potential–because the symbols used held differing meanings for client and therapist.

Regarding the therapist as "hearer," Tisdale (1992) suggests that each time a sermon is prepared, the preacher must decide whether to use his or her own frame of reference or that of the intended hearer. Kraft (1992) explains that since universal symbols for communicating across/among/ between cultures do not exist, we can adopt either an "extractionist" (speaker) or an "identificational" (hearer) perspective when communicating. The extractionist posture demands that the speaker's world view be used and that the listener first adopt that frame of reference. It could be argued that this is precisely what therapists do when they deliver a message which insists that the client first learn and adopt an entirely new vocabulary (that of the speaker).

On the other hand, the identificational perspective adopts the frame of reference of the listener. In this case, the "communicators become familiar with the conceptual framework of the receptor and attempt to fit their communication to the categories and felt needs of that frame of reference" (Kraft, 1992, p. 152). Combs and Freeman (1990) suggest two reasons why communicating from the perspective of the client is advantageous. First, clients can avoid becoming indoctrinated in the therapist's jargon;

second, strategies for change based on the hearer's frame of reference have a better chance of being carried out successfully. Thus, the effort to develop and deliver good sermons in therapy includes both a sensitivity to the clients' cultures and a willingness to adapt the way and the content of what we speak so as to be heard and understood by them.

Few messages, if any, should be assumed to have universal meaning. Because Scriptural illustrations are personal and can be interpreted in many ways, therapists should highlight the importance of making informed personal choices. The ability to make informed and reflective decisions without certain knowledge of future events defines our humanity. Although Scriptures may guide clients in the process of choice, ultimately each person is faced with the consequences of his or her decision-making. Ironically, clients may not be aware of what they are doing and thus not consider the consequences of their activity.

Packer (1985) describes three levels of activity: ready-to-hand, unready-to-hand, and present-at-hand. His contention is that most people go through life with ready-to-hand activity. Such activities do not require much reflection. For example, going to the mailbox to check the mail requires little or no reflection. An unready-to-hand activity requires problem-solving skills. If, for example, one were to walk to the mailbox and find that it had been knocked over, one would shift out of a ready-to-hand mind set and into an unready-to-hand mind set. As soon as the mailbox were securely set aright, one would probably return to a ready-to-hand frame of reference. Finally, present-at-hand activity is a reflective level of activity. Effective sermons in therapy may disrupt ready-to-hand activities and require clients to become reflective of their life choices. Such reflections help clients mediate conflicting goals. They may help clients make decisions based on an understanding of their choices. The value of reflective decision-making has been discussed relative to recent practice innovations (Sells, Smith, Coe, Yoshioka & Robbins 1994; Smith, Jenkins & Sells, 1995). It is often critical prior to resolving past hurts and avoiding impulsive decisions. However, the ability to be involved in present-at-hand activity may depend in part on clients' readiness for change.

Prochaska, DiClemente and Norcross (1992) examined clients readiness for change. They propose that three stages of readiness exist: precontemplative, contemplative, and action. Their contention is that in many instances clients' resistance is a function of their readiness for change. They assert that clients in a precontemplative state are unable to articulate their problems (and thus are unwilling to act to resolve them). Clients in the contemplative stage are able to articulate their problems but are ambivalent about change. And that clients in the action state are able to articulate their problems, are not paralyzed by ambivalence about change and thus are able to enact change with relatively little indecision. Assisting clients in moving through these stages is one of the tasks of the social worker. Good sermons which reframe and broaden perspectives can assist in moving clients into a stage of readiness.

Despite taking precautions, any therapeutic sermon may not have its intended effects. For example, clients may feel shame if therapeutic sermons inadvertently remind them of embarrassing or shameful behaviors. While shame-eliciting sermons can be a powerful incentive for change, such ploys may be disrespectful of clients. As opposed to reaching a superficial compliance with the therapist's requests, it is ultimately more important for clients to understand their choices and to be able to create a coherent decision-making schema.

CONCLUSION

Little is certain in life. Clients and therapists are both beset with making decisions about their lives. Sermons tap into stories that provide guidance, comfort, and warning for clients. Knowing how to deliver sermons is a critical set of skills for any therapist. Knowing which stories to deliver requires that therapists rely on their moral schema, practice wisdom, and humanity. The intangible mix of characteristics that defines our humanity also defines our practice. From this perspective, sermons help celebrate our humanity and include joys, sadness, frailty, and ultimately, serenity. The authors encourage continuing dialogue with representatives from a variety of fields, such as homiletics, that specialize in fashioning messages in order to communicate effectively with people. There seems to be much to gain from learning how to select words in such a way that clients can hear and understand them. If nothing more, such efforts can at least improve the relationship between client and social worker and maximally be a catalyst for positive change.

The notion that cultural "lenses" are an important consideration for therapists is not a new topic in clinical social work and family therapy. For example, Saba and Rodgers (1989) argue that drawing distinctions among cultures can either heal or harm. However, we contend that paying attention to a semiotic consideration of our clients' culture (or subculture) enhances the ability of therapists to fashion and deliver more effective sermons (i.e., messages) in a therapy session, especially when they are created using the elements of a good sermon.

REFERENCES

Breunlin, D. C., Schwartz, R. C., & MacKune-Karrer, B. M. (1992). *Metaframeworks: Transcending the models of family therapy*. San Francisco, CA: Jossey-Bass Inc.

Capps, D. (1990). *Reframing: A new method in pastoral care*. Minneapolis, MN: Augsburg Fortress.

Combs, G., & Freedman, J. (1990). *Symbol, story and ceremony: Using metaphor in individual and family therapy*. New York: Basic Books.

de Shazer, S., Berg, I. K., Lipchik, E., Nunnally, E., Molnar, A., Gingerich, W., & Weiner-Davis, M. (1986). Brief therapy: Focused solution development. *Family Process, 25*, 207-222.

Geertz, C. (1973). *The interpretation of cultures*. New York: Basic Books.

Haley, J. (1976). *Problem solving therapy*. San Francisco, CA: Jossey-Bass.

Kraft, C. H. (1992). *Christianity in culture: A study in dynamic Biblical theologizing in cross-cultural perspective*. Maryknoll, NY: Orbis Books.

Lankton, S. R., & Lankton, C. H. (1986). *Enchantment and intervention in family therapy*. New York: Brunner/Mazel.

Maruyama, M. (1977). Heterogenistics: An epistemological restructuring of biological and social sciences. *Cybernetica, 20*, 69-86.

Minuchin, S., & Fishman, H. C. (1981). *Family therapy techniques*. Cambridge, MA: Harvard University Press.

O'Hanlon, W. H., & Weiner-Davis, M. (1989). *In search of solutions: A new direction in psychotherapy*. New York: W. W. Norton.

Papp, P. (1984).The creative leap. *The Family Therapy Networker, 8* (5), 20-29.

Packer, M. J. (1985). Hermeneutic inquiry in the study of human contact. *American Psychologist, 40*(10), 1081-1093.

Perry, L. M. (1993). *A manual for Biblical preaching*. Grand Rapids, MI: Baker Book House.

Prochaska, J. O., DiClemente, C. C., & Norcross, J. C. (1992). In search of how people change: Applications to addictive behaviors. *American Psychologist, 47*(9), 1102-1114.

Saba, G., & Rodgers, D. V. (1989). Discrimination in urban family practice: Lessons from minority poor families. *Journal of Psychotherapy and the Family, 6*(1-2), 177-207.

Schreiter, R. J. (1986). *Constructing local theologies*. Maryknoll, NY: Orbis Books.

Sells, S. P., Smith, T. W., Coe, M. J., Yoshioka, M., & Robbins, J. (1994). An ethnography of couple and therapist experiences in reflecting team practice. *Journal of Marital and Family Therapy, 20*, 247-266.

Smith, T. E., & Counsell, S. (1991). Scripture as narrative and therapy. *Journal of Poetry Therapy, 8*, 149-163.

Smith, T. E., Jenkins, D. A., & Sells, S. P. (1995). Reflecting teams: Voices of diversity. *Journal of Family Psychotherapy, 6*(2), 49-70.

Tisdale, N. T. (1992). Preaching as local theology: A semiotic approach to congregational hermeneutics. Unpublished doctoral dissertation. Princeton Theological Seminary.

Index

Page numbers followed by f indicate figures.

Haworth
DOCUMENT DELIVERY
SERVICE

This valuable service provides a single-article order form for any article from a Haworth journal.

- *Time Saving:* No running around from library to library to find a specific article.
- *Cost Effective:* All costs are kept down to a minimum.
- *Fast Delivery:* Choose from several options, including same-day FAX.
- *No Copyright Hassles:* You will be supplied by the original publisher.
- *Easy Payment:* Choose from several easy payment methods.

Open Accounts Welcome for . . .
- Library Interlibrary Loan Departments
- Library Network/Consortia Wishing to Provide Single-Article Services
- Indexing/Abstracting Services with Single Article Provision Services
- Document Provision Brokers and Freelance Information Service Providers

---

MAIL or *FAX* THIS ENTIRE ORDER FORM TO:

Haworth Document Delivery Service
The Haworth Press, Inc.
10 Alice Street
Binghamton, NY 13904-1580

or **FAX:** 1-800-895-0582
or **CALL:** 1-800-342-9678
  9am-5pm EST

PLEASE SEND ME PHOTOCOPIES OF THE FOLLOWING SINGLE ARTICLES:

1) Journal Title: _____
   Vol/Issue/Year: _____Starting & Ending Pages:_____
   Article Title:_____
   _____

2) Journal Title: _____
   Vol/Issue/Year: _____Starting & Ending Pages:_____
   Article Title:_____
   _____

3) Journal Title: _____
   Vol/Issue/Year: _____Starting & Ending Pages:_____
   Article Title:_____
   _____

4) Journal Title: _____
   Vol/Issue/Year: _____Starting & Ending Pages:_____
   Article Title:_____

(See other side for Costs and Payment Information)

COSTS: Please figure your cost to order quality copies of an article.

1. Set-up charge per article: $8.00
   ($8.00 × number of separate articles)   _____

2. Photocopying charge for each article:
   1-10 pages: $1.00   _____

   11-19 pages: $3.00   _____

   20-29 pages: $5.00   _____

   30+ pages: $2.00/10 pages   _____

3. Flexicover (optional): $2.00/article   _____

4. Postage & Handling: US: $1.00 for the first article/
   $.50 each additional article   _____

   Federal Express: $25.00   _____

   Outside US: $2.00 for first article/
   $.50 each additional article   _____

5. Same-day FAX service: $.35 per page   _____

   GRAND TOTAL: _____

METHOD OF PAYMENT: (please check one)

❑ Check enclosed   ❑ Please ship and bill. PO # _____
(sorry we can ship and bill to bookstores only! All others must pre-pay)

❑ Charge to my credit card: ❑ Visa;   ❑ MasterCard;   ❑ Discover;
❑ American Express;

Account Number: _____ Expiration date: _____

Signature: ✗ _____

Name: _____ Institution: _____

Address: _____

_____

City: _____ State: _____ Zip: _____

Phone Number: _____ FAX Number: _____

MAIL or *FAX* THIS ENTIRE ORDER FORM TO:

Haworth Document Delivery Service | **or FAX:** 1-800-895-0582
The Haworth Press, Inc. | **or CALL:** 1-800-342-9678
10 Alice Street | .   9am-5pm EST)
Binghamton, NY 13904-1580